Treasures of Chinese
Qing Dynasty Palace Glass

Treasures of Chinese Qing Dynasty Palace Glass

Liu Xinyan,
Xiang Xiaoqun,
Zhong Guomiao

PHOTOGRAPHY BY
Lian Xu

UNICORN

Published in 2019 by
Unicorn, an imprint of Unicorn Publishing Group LLP
5 Newburgh Street
London
W1F 7RG
www.unicornpublishing.org

ISBN 978 1 911604 87 7

10 9 8 7 6 5 4 3 2 1

Translated by Sarah Waldram

Designed by Nick Newton Design

Printed in Turkey by Jellyfish

CONTENTS

DIFFERENT TASTES IN GLASS

WANG LUXIANG

The world is unimaginable without glass.

We are accustomed to being surrounded by glass, from the vast glass facades of skyscrapers, to glass cabinets, bottles and tableware, and, at the smaller end of the scale, lenses for spectacles and glass beads. Without glass, we could not live.

In fact, the changes that glass has brought to us go much further than these objects. It has also been a tool for enabling human thought to change the world. From the prism, we learnt that sunlight was a multi-coloured mix of different wavelengths, and understood the mystery of colour. The concave-convex lens not only enlarges and shrinks objects, but can also bring images closer and push them away. So humans invented spectacles to solve vision problems, enabling the shortsighted to see things at a distance and the longsighted to focus on objects nearby. As a result, the number of years an individual could spend on reading, learning and doing meticulous work was greatly extended, such that the opportunity to acquire knowledge and do advanced craftsmanship also substantially increased. So, the proportion of people able to enter the intellectual elite and become excellent craftsmen rose considerably, and the ability of humans to acquire knowledge and high-level skills made an unprecedented improvement. It is as if the intelligent life-form of humanity, with the help of glass, gave its intellect wings. In particular, the ordinary telescope, astronomical telescope and microscope, all based on the optical lens, extended the range and fields of observation, to the outside world, the cosmos and the microscopic. The explosion of knowledge created by this change enabled humanity, in the Middle Ages, to step into an era of modern science and technology. Thus, glass has not only been a tool for us to observe world, but also a tool to change the world.

When glass was first developed, however, it did not have this role. Its function was to please human beings with its glorious colour, as an elegant and radiant aesthetic object. Moreover, through the study of the status and use of glass in the world's major cultures, anthropologists show that many cultures either had no glass, or restricted its utilization to appreciation of its gorgeous colours. Only Europe developed in the direction of creation of colourless and transparent glass. In other cultures, the large-scale accumulation of reliable knowledge did not occur, and there was no explosion of knowledge to lead human beings to a society with modern science and technology. China was one such culture.

Why did such differences exist? Why did glass have such a different evolutionary fate in different cultures?

In the view of Alan Macfarlane, professor of anthropology at the University of Cambridge, there were many reasons, the fundamental one being differing approaches towards glass between European and other cultures. He believes that the Romans endowed glass with a certain significance, such that it became an important object. Because of this, the history of glass in western Europe was separate from that of Asia. Professor Macfarlane thinks that the revolution in the Romans' approach to glass was a key feature in the development of European glass history.

The long history of glass originates in the part of Asia known as the Middle East. Glass-making technology developed along the east side of Mediterranean, where it was discovered and then spread to the Greek islands and North Africa by Phoenician traders, finally attaining glorious achievements in ancient Egypt. Perhaps in about 500 BCE, the technology was brought to East Asia and the Chinese learnt the skill. So, by around 100 BCE, people in most regions of Eurasia had some basic knowledge of producing coloured and plain glass. However, apart from in western Europe, glass was merely regarded as a substitute for more precious materials (gems, jade, agate and amber, for instance), and used for jewelry and luxury receptacles.

Only in Rome, the use of glass developed in new directions. Important examples include the semi-transparent and opaque coloured glass pieces used for mosaic murals, and the transparent glass used for wine vessels. The former architectural use in turn led to the coloured stained glass of the medieval Catholic Church. Furthermore, the coloured windows of the church directly inspired the popularity of the clear, flat glass windows used domestically. Thus, the manufacture of glass started to have a function in everyday life. Production capacity developed by leaps and bounds. During the Renaissance, the creation of window glass became a key industry in some European cities. Glass became an industrial product, contributing to the Industrial Revolution in Europe, and creating a great deal of wealth for society. The latter wine vessel use was initially intended merely for enjoyment of the charming colour of wine, and the appraisal of its quality. But, in pursuit of transparency, crystal glass was then invented in Venice. This then promoted the development of optical glass, with a contribution to the history of human science and technology that cannot be overestimated. The new directions for the development of glass originating in Rome were determined by an approach that respected the material property of glass itself, in other words an understanding of the power of glass as a distinctive and important substance.

One summer vacation, my wife and I did an academic study tour, taking in Venice, Florence, Rome and Cambridge. Although our object was not glass-related, interestingly, we could not help but be deeply impressed by the dazzling shapes and colours of the glass products that fill the multitude of shops on the streets of Venice, and by the romance of the world's capital of glass art. Without glass, there would be no Venice. In Palazzo Medici Riccardi, in Florence, prompted by my wife, I took note of the transparent patterned glass set in the ancient windows of the thick stone walls, probably the earliest domestic flat colourless window glass in the world. Tourists might not appreciate that these ordinary glass windows had a much more extended and deeper influence in the development of civilization than, say, mural painting or public statuary. At the Galileo Museum, also in Florence, there was a small exhibition hall filled with the earliest glass containers used for experimental science. Owing to these strangely shaped glass cups, bottles and tubes, some with long necks, some with round bellies, modern chemistry and pharmacy began.

At the Museo Nazionale Romano – Palazzo Massimo alle Terme, near Rome railway station, there were many mural remains from the ruins of the Roman empire, uncovered during archaeological excavations, some of which were set with coloured glass pieces. We could see that this colourful glass, with its complex and varied patterns, was produced specifically for these mosaics, which were in such high demand. The glass mosaics were not only a feature of palaces and the homes of rich people, but also of public bathhouses and arcades. Moreover, the museum had on display a glass twisted, coloured bowl of the Roman period, perfectly preserved, with patterns like tortoiseshell, luster and amber. In a mural at the Villa di Livia, built 2000 years ago, I saw a still-life painting showing a large transparent glass bowl with a group of brown bottles in it. Through the colourless wall of the bowl, the bottles are clearly visible. Thus, at that time in Rome, transparent glass was used not only for producing wine glasses, but also for this kind of large bowl for cooling wine bottles.

At King's College Chapel, in Cambridge, Professor Macfarlane pointed out the lofty church windows, telling us about the astonishing role of stained glass in Gothic church architecture. In the tearoom in the orchard of his home on the outskirts of Cambridge, he offered us tea in the Chinese Gongfu tradition according to an improved Japanese tea ceremony, and gave me a signed copy of *The Glass Bathyscaphe: How Glass Changed the World*, which he wrote with Gerry Martin.

It was a fantastic trip, which was supposed to have nothing to do with glass, but in the end could not be separated from it. All these illustrations show that the world has indeed been improved by glass. The story of glass, hidden away in the history of human civilization, showed up in places quite beyond our expectation, encountered by chance, as a pleasant surprise.

One wonderful evening I came across the collection of glass objects from the Qing-period (1644–1912) palace belonging to Mr Liu Xinyan and the Jipin Jingshe husband-and-wife team, Zhong Guomiao and Xiang Xiaoqun, and it brought me unexpected pleasure. Their collection has been going for many years. It is unnecessary to detail the hard work and bittersweet tales of their travels around the world, since many collectors have had such experiences. But readers can find exquisite, splendid and excellent artefacts in this book. Description here is superfluous – what I want to convey is how to learn about glass, a substance we think we know.

There is no certain answer as to when East Asian culture as represented by China started to use and produce glass. There is archaeological evidence to show that China had glass products in the form of sacrificial vessels from the Western Zhou period (c. 1045–771 BCE). Some experts believe that the technique for producing this kind of glass originated from the Middle East, while others advocate that Chinese glass technology originated independently, since the components and composition of early Chinese glass are different to glass of the Middle East. There are early prehistoric sculptures in unofficial collections, including those of animals and human beings. Some of these are large, over a foot in height: these are carvings of natural glass. Traces of volcanic lava and other rock can be seen clearly through the transparent glass. Analysis shows this is concretionary natural glass that prehistoric human beings collected in areas of volcanic eruption. They treated it as jade, and carved it into primitive totems, in keeping with the principle that 'the beautiful stone is jade'. This is the earliest use of glass by human beings, though the glass in question was natural.

Common archaeological artefacts in the Changsha region are glass *bi* (discs) of the Warring States period, which imitate the texture, colour and shape of jade, and were used for burial.

The most famous discoveries are the so-called 'dragonfly eye' glass beads, whose complicated wrapped-wire glass technology was influenced by West Asia and highly developed in China. Up until the present day, they are pursued by collectors worldwide as the highest quality beads.

Along the overland Silk Road and Maritime Silk Route, the glass products of Rome, Damascus and Persia continuously entered China. From the Han (206 BCE–220 CE) through to the Tang (610–907) periods, the flow was unbroken. Glass represents powerful evidence of the cultural communication between China and the Western world. Exotic glass products had a very high status in China and became luxuries for high society and eminent monks. The main reason for this might be that Chinese glass-producing skills had languished. Regardless of the splendid or beautiful nature of glass, the product did not have a commercial space for large-scale development in a civilization with the custom of consuming hot drinks and a strong ceramics industry. Furthermore, since Chinese civilization regarded jade as exemplifying beauty, in terms of both cultural psychology and value, glass (even if there was the lofty notion of 'glass light' in Buddhism) would never challenge the gentle and sincere aesthetic tradition of Confucianism. The aesthetic tendency of the Chinese people, nurtured by a jade culture thousands of years old, shaped the Chinese approach to glass. That approach did not respect the unique material properties of glass, but saw it only as an alternative to jade (and other gemstones like jade), or porcelain (porcelain too was regarded as similar to jade). The more it could imitate, the more value it had. So, when the Silk Road came to be interrupted, there was no value to a local glass manufacturing industry. The court did not require it, and, in other parts of society, only the Boshan area of Shandong still used a local traditional formula and techniques to produce low-quality glass.

So, when Westerners came to China again towards the end of the Ming period (1368–1644) and start of the Qing, while the glass industry had been flourishing in western Europe, in China it had almost gone back to square one. With the help of European missionaries, Guangzhou, that is the South, became the new base for glass-making. And notably, with the support of the Kangxi emperor (*reg.* 1661–1722), the Qing palace workshops in Beijing set up a glass-producing plant in 1696, located beside the French missionary Catholic church at Chanchikou, probably to the north of present-day Zhongnanhai. Missionaries Jean de Fontaney and Kilian Stumpf worked here, and two glass artisans, Vilette and d'Andign, were recruited from France. During the period of the Qianlong emperor (*reg.* 1735–96), the court employed two further missionaries in the glass plant: Gabriel-Leonard de Brossard and Pierre d'Incarville. Apprentices from two Chinese glass-producing centres, the town of Yanshen in Boshan in Shandong and Guangzhou, received training in the more complex glass-blowing technology. They could blow large glass items expertly. Moreover, they learnt to sculpt glass and to create coloured glass, as well as techniques for engraving and polishing, using wheels from Kilian Stumpf. There were seventeen rooms in the glass workshop-plant, which was divided into two parts: one part comprised the kiln rooms for producing and blowing glass, while the other housed the grinding and carving rooms for exquisite cold working.

The organization of work in the glass-making plant was similar to that in other institutions within the Qing workshops. Usually the emperor gave orders directly, with precise instructions on the glass-making, as well as supervising the whole production process. Meanwhile, the head of glass factory would direct the craftsmen to do the work as a team.

There were four main types of glass product made at the glass factory in the workshops. The first was imperial daily supplies, including glass cups, bowls, glasses, plates, pots, boxes, snuff bottles, rinsing utensils, brush pots and pen racks. The second was decorative objects, such as glass vases, flower pots, lamps, bracelets and belts. The third was items used in sacrifices, for example glass beads, censers, vases and bowls. And the fourth was objects given as gifts.

Outlay relating to glassware production at the workshop-factory was huge. According to records relating to the workshops at the Hall of Mental Cultivation (Yangxin Dian) within the imperial palace dating to 1752, for the purpose of producing 22 items of glass, the kiln was kept alight for 113 days, from 20 November one year to 13 March the following one. 4,500 *jin* of firewood were used each day, and 508,500 *jin* in all. A sum of 1,118.7 *taels* of silver was spent on firewood alone, and when combined with other materials the total cost was 3,349.127 *taels* of silver, that is about 30,000 to 40,000 Chinese *yuan* for producing each item in today's money. This represented the height of expense, and demonstrated a complete disregard for cost.

It is said that the motive for Kangxi to establish the glass factory was that, when he first succeeded to the throne, he had been impressed by glassware from Italy and Holland. The exotic glass with its luxurious craftwork deeply impressed the young emperor, arousing his curiosity and ambition, and he became determined to set up glass factory at the Qing court.

Under the supervision of the emperor, and through the efforts of the missionaries and Chinese craftsmen, finally, the glass factory produced glassware that satisfied the emperor and could be considered for use at state ceremonies and giving as gifts.

In 1721, Kangxi sent 136 pieces of 'Beijing glass' to the Pope.

In the list of gifts presented by the Kangxi emperor to the King of Portugal in 1722, there were: two red glass dishes, eight glass cups in a colour described as 'the sky after a shower', ten small blue saucers, ten medium red glass dishes, five glass cups white on the inside and gilded on the outside, two coloured glass pots decorated with Chinese-style patterns and people, two 'the sky after a shower'-coloured glass dishes, two white-patterned glass saucers and two white-patterned glass covers. The glass items totaled 43 pieces in all.

On 28 April 1722, Kangxi sent the Tsar eighty-six large carved glass cups, in four colours: yellow, white, blue and green.

According to the statistics, in the year 1722, the Qing court presented 264 pieces from the glass factory to envoys of various countries.

Thus, the glass products from the workshop glass factory, that is the Chinese imperial glass plant, eventually satisfied the demands of the emperor, winning his favour through realizing quality, technique and design. Kangxi sent Chinese-made glassware to the monarchs of European countries, enabling him to project a degree of ambition and confidence. Twenty years after the construction of glass factory, it was producing high-quality products that did not embarrass the country. Prior to this it had really experienced many failures!

It is said that the Kangxi emperor had the habit, every other day, of appreciating the glassware and glazed objects in the Hall of Mental Cultivation, proudly comparing them with European glass products. When he visited Suzhou during his journey to the South, he gave seventeen items of glassware to a favoured official, Song Luo. Meanwhile, another favourite, Gao Shiqi, was rewarded by Kangxi with twenty pieces of glass, after he remarked to the emperor, 'The glass we now produce far outstrips that of the Western world.'

Gao Shiqi's words should not be seen merely as intended to please the emperor. In terms of production system, scale, technology and variety, there was, of course, a very great difference between glass production at the Chinese royal court and in western Europe. But, if looked at from the perspective of luxury goods, court glassware in the periods of the Kangxi, Yongzheng (*reg.* 1723–35) and Qianlong emperors was indeed some of the best according to the aesthetic criteria of delicacy, beauty and craft, quite apart from putting a value on cost, manpower, material resources and time. This glassware achieved a standard that had never been approached previously and would never occur again. Among the products, some reached an acme of perfection, for example, in the Kangxi period, the glassware described as ruby, gold-flecked red and 'the sky after a shower', and, in the Qianlong period, silver-flecked blue glass.

In particular, the unique Chinese styles of surface relief glass and painted enamel glass meant that glass production at the Qing court broke away from an emphasis on the particular material characteristics of glass, abandoning the valuable qualities of transparency, malleability and plasticity. Instead, these were compromised by use of the cold processing technology of gemstone and jade, and surrendered to fine painting. Thus, a working process that could have been completed quickly became very long. Time and cost rose out of all proportion. Glass products gained added value by the use of these other techniques. Thus, missionaries at the time believed that the emperor's intention in establishing the glass factory was only to satisfy himself, and to add a new unique substance in the range of luxury goods, not that he had a commercial purpose. Consequently, glass products became smaller, and the pursuit of colour outdistanced the interest in transparency. Overall, glass products moved from transparent in the Kangxi period, to semi-transparent and opaque in the Yongzheng period, to opaque in Qianlong period. Furthermore, in pursuit of adding luxury value, notably the value associated with added processing, the time and cost involved in engraving and painting was extended to the maximum. For this reason, the price of glass items painted with enamel and those with surface relief were the highest among Qing court glass products on the market.

Why did the main glass products move from blown and coloured transparent glass in Kangxi period, to engraved and painted glass processed cold? And why did they gradually become more opaque?

The reasons are complicated, but it was partly a cultural approach that led to adopting this strategy.

The Kangxi emperor invited many missionaries to China, and to his palace. He was very interested in, and a student of, Western culture, especially science and technology. Although he did not convert his personal interest into public policy, at court at least, among his twenty-seven other factories, he established a glass factory. He allowed foreign missionaries to run this factory and to teach Chinese craftspeople. The production team was mainly foreign missionaries, so, of course, most of the products were designed and produced according to the traditional glass techniques of western Europe. This was the reason why the main glass products were blown and transparent ones in the Kangxi period.

The Yongzheng emperor expelled the missionaries. His cultural character and aesthetic taste were more domestic, or, we could say, more purist and closed, as reflected in general in the decorative arts of this period. His character and taste also affected glass products. What is more, the Yongzheng court no longer had experienced missionaries guiding work at the glass factory. As a result, in terms of the workers, the factory had to change to use Chinese techniques and rely more heavily on the craftsmen of the jade and enamel factories. So, the deep-rooted jade culture with its many-thousand-year history started to pervade the glass production technology that had come from the Western world. At the emperor's disposal, excellent workers in the jade and enamel factories took a hand in the now missionary-less glass factory. Thus, Chinese culture overwhelmed the overseas glass production skills. The 'Sinicization' of the glass production process was completed during the Yongzheng period. When the Qianlong emperor acceded, although he employed two experienced missionaries to take charge of the glass factory, the best he could do was to follow what had come before and make it more perfect. His own style had a strong impact on the production of glass. Furthermore, through the efforts of his father and grandfather, glass-production skills were at the highest level in Qianlong period. But the style became even more complex, with greater decoration, and the aesthetic taste in glass did not return to the state of focusing on its own unique character, but moved in the direction of enhancing the value of glass material more even more intensely. Decorative techniques, such as cutting, engraving and painting, became more and more involved.

At this juncture, I would like to add just a little more about the painting of glass with enamel at the Qing palace, to help explain why this kind of snuff bottle so costly.

Glass-body enamelling is a kind of glaze technology, which involves, first, mixing glass powder into a flux, along with oil, honey or tree gum, and applying this (the frit) with a paintbrush in coloured patterns on a glass container at room temperature. Then, this is heated until the fluxing agent makes the glaze flow, finally hardening and melding with the container. The most difficult part of this technique is control, since it is an extremely difficult task to melt glaze on the surface of a glass object, even more so than on copperware and porcelain. Owing to the low melting point of glass, the glaze can be applied only at a relatively low temperature. But usually, the fusion temperatures of glaze and the main glass object differ only by a few degrees. So, to avoid the glassware softening or becoming deformed, and yet to achieve the melting and then setting of the glaze on it, it is quite an uncertain undertaking, requiring craftsmen with much experience. Depending on the precise sintering point of the various glazes, the fritting process was divided into several stages. Moreover, the difficulty in heat control increases as the size of the glass item increases. Therefore, the glass painted enamel technology of the Qing period focused almost exclusively on small glass containers like snuff bottles. So, we can see why a glass-body painted enamel snuff bottle created at the Qing court becomes priceless. The first reason is its scarcity, the second is the complexity of the exquisite techniques involved, the third is the high artistic quality, and the fourth is the immeasurable human effort and time spent on its production, from seeking the raw material to melting, shaping, polishing, painting and sintering. These are the essential characteristics of the Qing palace glass. All these characteristics, however, deviate from the direction of industrialization, commercialization, popularization and daily use. So the development direction of glass industry in China was totally different to the one that existed from the sixteenth century in the Western world.

In 1742, the Qianlong emperor, who had been in power for seven years, visited the workshop glass factory with the new missionaries Gabriel-Leonard de Brossard and Pierre d'Incarville and other officials, and put forward a plan to improve the level of glass production. Ten years later, in response to the request to enlarge the scale of production at the glass factory, Qianlong ordered the construction of a hugely expensive kiln. Glass-making at the Qing Court had reached its highpoint. With the death of Brossard and d'Incarville in 1757 and 1758, the workshop glass factory started to go into decline. In 1760, when Qianlong realized that there was no-one proficient at glass-making among the missionaries employed by Qing court, he was deeply disappointed. Another decade passed, and Qianlong ordered a glass lamp to be mended, but the craftsmen at glass factory could not repair it. A further twenty years later, a scientist in a diplomatic team dispatched by the British monarchy wrote in his report that there was a glass factory in Beijing that had been managed and guided by missionaries, but it seemed there was no-one taking care of it now …

Owing to the difficulty of the firing process for the manufacture of enamel-painted glass, its success-rate is extremely low, and such pieces are rare. These artefacts represent the highest level of craftsmanship and artistry of their time. Coloured enamel-painted glassware was an art treasure monopolized by the palace. From its beginnings to its decline, it was confined to the court, used only by the emperor and simply not encountered by ordinary people.

ENAMEL-PAINTED GLASS

Opaque-white-ground blue glass snuff bottle with landscape-and-figure continuous scene painted in enamel

Period: Qing Kangxi
Inscription: Made in the Qing period
Dimensions: h. 53.6 mm

This snuff bottle is vase-shaped, with an open mouth and circular foot. The bottom is inscribed in brown regular script *Da Qing nian zhi* ('Made in the Qing period'). The opaque-white ground is painted with a landscape-and-figure continuous scene in blue-glass enamel. The jade-like pure white base has blue glaze applied, just like blue-and-white porcelain. The painted surface of the object is shaded, making stronger and weaker light distinct, in layers of wash, imitating exactly blue-and-white porcelain. The craftsman uses the colouring technique skilfully, consciously presenting many layers of different tones, so that in just a few strokes he conveys a brushwork rhythm moving between light and dark. Distant mountains and foreground, pavilions, terraces and towers, all are richly layered and three-dimensional. The use of the method of unifying and integration is close to the expression of traditional Chinese ink painting, in typical Kangxi-period (1661–1722) style. Kangxi-period coloured enamel is rare, so this object is very valuable.

Transparent glass long-necked vase with bamboo-and-plum design painted in multicoloured enamel

Period: Qing
Inscription: Made in the Qianlong era
Dimensions: h. 155 mm

This vase has a long neck and a round belly. The bottom is inscribed in seal script traced in gold *Qianlong nian zhi* ('Made in the Qianlong era'). The bamboo–plum painting on the vase was a common theme for palace objects, implying a personal character that is 'lofty, unsullied and noble'. The fact that the inscription is traced in gold, in contrast to the general use of blue glass for inscriptions, adds to the value of the object.

The vase is transparent white, and was blown. The body of the vase has an obvious blowing scar mark, and its slightly irregular shape is a genuine indication of the glass-blowing technology under the Qianlong emperor (*reg* 1735–96). Owing to the difficulty of enamelled glass production, most pieces are small snuff bottle. Of the twenty or so items of enamelled glass in the Palace Museum, Beijing, only a handful are vases, and the remainder snuff bottles. Comparatively speaking, in the context of enamelled glass, this long-necked vase constitutes a large piece, and is rare.

Opaque white glass snuff bottle with all-over flowers painted in enamel

Period: Qing
Inscription: Made in the Yongzheng era
Dimensions: h. 42.8 mm, mouth outer diam. 14.1 mm, mouth inner diam. 7.8 mm

This snuff bottle is in the shape of a flat bottle, with an oval foot. The bottom is inscribed in regular script in blue glass *Yongzheng nian zhi* ('Made in the Yongzheng era'). The opaque white glass base is round and smooth, and the body is painted all over with flowers of varying sizes, with no gaps. This is known as *baihua bu luodi* ('a hundred flowers cover the base'). The bottle uses fresh and elegant colours, in an intricate design that is not over-complicated. The individual flowers are glazed delicately and lightly, in a rich variety of colours, probably with early imported glaze, in a refined style that is fluent and natural. In the Qianlong era, the colour of *baihua bu luodi* pieces was to become magnificent, but it lost this freshness and elegance.

Coloured enamel of the Yongzheng era (1723–35) is extremely unusual and precious. As far as we know, there is only a snuff bottle in the shape of a segment of bamboo in the National Palace Museum, Taipei. The value of this snuff bottle can be imagined.

Opaque white glass gold-ground snuff bottle with riches-and-honour design painted in enamel

Period: Qing
Inscription: Made in the Qianlong era
Dimensions: h. 51.2 mm, mouth outer diam. 15.7 mm, mouth inner diam. 8 mm

This snuff bottle is in the shape of a flat bottle, with an oval foot. The opaque-white glass base is applied with coloured enamel on a gold ground. The two sides of the bottle have petal-shaped panels. Within the panel on one side are painted hibiscus and osmanthus, while the panel on the other has plum blossom and camellia. This implies 'riches and honour'. Outside the panels are painted twining branches of flowers. The bottom is inscribed in seal script in blue glass *Qianlong nian zhi* ('Made in the Qianlong era'). A gold and lapis lazuli lid has an ivory spoon attached.

The bottle is decorated with a gold ground throughout, and the overall appearance is elegant and rich. It displays the grandeur of items used in the imperial household, and is a typical creation of the glass factory at the palace workshops. The Palace Museum, Beijing, has only three snuff bottles approaching this one in decoration and demonstrating comparable skill.

Opaque white glass snuff bottle with stone-and-orchid painted in enamel

Period: Qing
Inscription: Made in the Qianlong era
Dimensions: h. 53.7 mm

Opaque white glass snuff bottle with stone-and-peony painted in enamel

Period: Qing
Inscription: Made in the Qianlong era
Dimensions: h. 59.6 mm, mouth outer diam. 19.8 mm, mouth inner diam. 8 mm

This snuff bottle is in the shape of a flat bottle, with a level bottom and no foot. The bottom is inscribed in regular script *Qianlong nian zhi* ('Made in the Qianlong era'). Owing to prolonged use, the inscription is faint and indistinct. On the opaque white ground, coloured enamel is applied. The bottle is painted on one side with stones and plants, and a poem in the emperor's calligraphy written on the other. While poems in the emperor's calligraphy are reasonably common on porcelain, on enamelled glass they are very rare.

烁雨霏霏
碧蘚滋閒愔
今日步東籬不
如泠夜寒朝裏
開到卤風第
幾枝

Opaque white glass snuff bottle with gourd-vine painted in multicoloured enamel

Period: Qing
Inscription: Made in the Qianlong era
Dimensions: h. 51.6 mm, mouth outer diam. 12.8 mm, mouth inner diam. 7 mm

This snuff bottle is in the shape of a gourd, with a straight mouth, two handles, accentuated waist and concave bottom. The bottom is inscribed in seal script in red glass *Qianlong nian zhi* ('Made in the Qianlong era'). On the opaque-white glass a yellow ground and coloured enamel are applied, and the whole body is painted with luxuriant gourd vines. The big gourd has nine small gourds carved on it. The long tendrils of the gourd vine symbolize continuity, implying 'many sons and many blessings', and the emperor's territory stretching out into the beyond.

The snuff bottle is exquisitely painted in brilliant colours. The three-dimensionality given by the carving enhances the visual effect. The yellow ground is symbolic of power. The inscription on the bottom is vigorous. It is a masterpiece of the palace workshops.

Opaque white glass snuff bottle with panel depicting mother-and-child painted in enamel

Period: Qing
Inscription: Made in the Qianlong era
Dimensions: h. 49.8 mm

This snuff bottle is in the shape of an octagonal flat bottle, with a level bottom. The bottom is inscribed in regular script in blue glass *Qianlong nian zhi* ('Made in the Qianlong era'). The front and back of the bottle are raised, and painted with representations of Occidental mother-and-child figures.

The depictions on the bottle are done by a court painter in imitation of Western style, and the shape is novel. Similar kinds of pictures found on snuff bottles at the Palace Museum, Beijing, are in the same vein.

Opaque white glass snuff bottle with goats symbolizing good fortune painted in enamel

Period: Qing
Inscription: Made in the Qianlong era
Dimensions: h. 51.2 mm, mouth outer diam. 15.7 mm, mouth inner diam. 8 mm

This snuff bottle is in the shape of a Guanyin vase, with a circular foot. The bottom is inscribed in regular script in blue glass *Qianlong nian zhi* ('Made in the Qianlong era'). The opaque-white glass base is painted in coloured enamel. The bottle depicts a continuous scene of three goats (three *yang*) playing in the mountains, implying 'the New Year (three *Yang* – a homonym) brings prosperity'. The base of the bottle is a pure and radiant white, and the composition ingenious and original. The three goats' features are vivid, and they look around in a lively manner. The glazed enamel is rich in colour, and it represents a rare masterpiece in enamel-painted glass.

Opaque white glass snuff bottle with landscape-and-figure continuous scene painted in enamel

Period: Qing
Inscription: Guyue Xuan
Dimensions: h. 61 mm

This snuff bottle is in the shape of a Guanyin vase, with a circular foot. The bottom is inscribed in red glass *Guyue Xuan* ('Ancient Moon Pavilion'). The opaque-white glass base is painted in coloured enamel, depicting a continuous scene of landscape and figures. To accurately convey landscape and figures, pavilions, terraces and towers, in such a limited space, is no mean feat.

The bottle depicts *Qiushan fangyou tu* ('Visiting Friends in the Autumnal Mountains'). The foreground shows a retreat in the mountains surrounded by streams, with a few friends wandering through it, and houses scattered among the tall pine trees. In the distance are steep mountains and broad rivers, with boats sailing on them. At the foot of the mountains, paths wind and interconnect. The sky is lofty and the clouds are light – the whole scene evokes a strong sense of autumn. This painting takes a method of the Yuan period (1279–1368), and possesses the vigorous style of the four Wangs of the early Qing. It displays extraordinary skill, embodying the superb technique of the court craftsmen. This is an unusual and fine piece.

Opaque white glass rinsing bowl with figure-and-landscape continuous scene design painted in enamel
Period: Qing
Inscription: Made in the Qianlong era
Dimensions: h. 47 mm

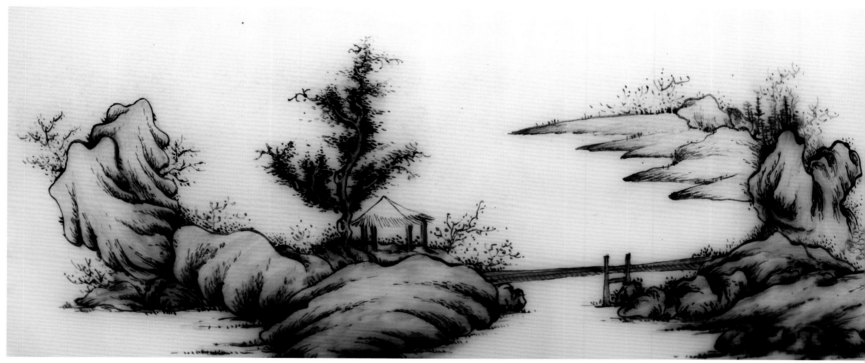

Milk-white glass hat-feather tube with cloud-and-bat design painted in enamel

Period: Qing
Inscription: Made in the Qianlong era
Dimensions: h. 75.8 mm

This hat-feather tube is long and slender. At one end, there is an eye that has a cord running through it with a gold bat attached. The edge of the eye it is inscribed in seal script in blue glass *Qianlong nian zhi* ('Made in the Qianlong era'). At the other end of the tube is a socket. The tube was used for holding a peacock feather, worn exclusively by officials of rank five and above. The hat-feather tube is an object unique to the Qing dynasty. Qing dynasty ranks were complex and strict, and the wearing of the peacock feature was not only a mark of degree of power, but also a symbol of honour, status and wealth. Thus, the emperor was sparing in granting peacock feathers to ministers. In the more than a hundred and seventy years from the Qianlong era to the end of the dynasty, there were only seven ministers who received the three-eyed peacock feather.

This hat-feather tube is enamel-painted with clouds and red bats (*hong fu*), implying 'great fortune (*hong fu*) reaches the heavens'. The colour-enamelled tube is extremely unusual and belongs to the category of rarities.

Opaque white glass snuff bottle with relief egret-and-lotus painted in enamel

Period: Qing
Inscription: Guyue Xuan
Dimensions: h. 48 mm

This snuff bottle is in the shape of a flat bottle, with an oval foot. The bottom is inscribed in blue glass *Guyue Xuan* ('Ancient Moon Pavilion'). It is opaque-white glass painted in coloured enamel. The body has a continuous scene of lotus pond and golden bird in high relief and painted in enamel. The blooming lotus flowers set off the green leaves, giving the bottle an irresistible freshness and elegance.

Opaque white glass vase-shaped snuff bottle with ball-flower design painted in enamel

Period: Qing
Inscription: Guyue Xuan
Dimensions: h. 61.7 mm, mouth outer diam. 16 mm, mouth inner diam. 8.6 mm

This snuff bottle is in the shape of a lantern vase, with a circular foot. The bottom is inscribed in blue glass *Guyue Xuan* ('Ancient Moon Pavilion'). It is opaque-white glass painted in coloured enamel. It is painted with a continuous ball-flower design, bearing a very close resemblance to the artefact shown on page 74. It is a treasure of palace imperial production.

Opaque white glass gold-ground snuff bottle with orchid design painted in enamel

Period: Qing
Inscription: Made in the Qianlong era
Dimensions: h. 50.7 mm, mouth outer diam. 15.5 mm, mouth inner diam. 8.1 mm

Opaque white glass snuff bottle with relief pheasant-and-peony design painted in multicoloured enamel
Period: Qing
Inscription: Guyue Xuan
Dimensions: h. 56.7 mm, mouth outer diam. 17.2 mm, mouth inner diam. 8.1 mm

Opaque white glass snuff bottle with relief dragon holding magic fungus painted in enamel

Period: Qing

Inscription: Guyue Xuan

Dimensions: h. 50 mm, mouth outer diam. 15 mm, mouth inner diam. 8 mm

Transparent glass lidded-bowl shaped snuff bottle with lotus-leaf design painted in enamel

Period: Qing
Inscription: Made in the Qianlong era
Dimensions: h. 44.5 mm, mouth outer diam. 12.1 mm, mouth inner diam. 6.5 mm

This snuff bottle is shaped like a lidded bowl, with a circular flared foot. The bottom is inscribed in regular script in blue glass *Qianlong nian zhi* ('Made in the Qianlong era'). The transparent glass base is painted in coloured enamel. The upper part of the bottle has a pearl-and-jade necklace pattern. The lower part depicts a continuous lotus-pond scene, evoking the atmosphere of high summer. It is an exquisite enamel-painted work.

Opaque white glass crabapple-cluster shaped snuff bottle with stone-and-chrysanthemum panel painted in enamel

Period: Qing
Inscription: Guyue Xuan
Dimensions: h. 52.1 mm

This snuff bottle is in the shape of a crabapple cluster, with a rounded foot. The bottom is inscribed in blue glass *Guyue Xuan* ('Ancient Moon Pavilion'). It is opaque-white glass painted in coloured enamel.

Both sides of the bottle have crabapple-shaped panels, inside which are painted stones and plants. Such distinctively crabapple-shaped snuff bottles are rare, and very attractive.

Opaque-white-ground blue glass knife handle with landscape-and-figure continuous scene painted in enamel

Period: Qing
Inscription: Made in the Qianlong era
Dimensions: h. 295 mm

The Qianlong emperor held weapons in high esteem, especially swords and knives. From the thirteenth to the twenty-second years of his reign (1748–57), the Qing palace workshops spared no effort in catering to Qianlong's tastes, producing a number of exquisitely crafted and richly decorated bladed weapons. Moreover, the emperor also explicitly ordered the production of knives, such as this one, to wear at his waist on important celebrations. Today, most of these are housed in the Palace Museum, Beijing. This knife was forged from fine steel, and centuries later remains gleaming and sharp. It is inscribed in regular script inlaid with gold *Qianlong nian zhi* ('Made in the Qianlong era'). The handle is made of milk-white glass, and is enamel-painted in blue glass with a continuous landscape, figure and Occidental-style architecture scene. The top of the handle is similarly inscribed *Qianlong nian zhi*, but in seal script in blue glass. It is rare to see two different types of inscription on a single object. The blue glass colour is soft, elegant and fresh. The handle is narrow: to accurately represent the landscape, figure and buildings in such a small space reflects the superb painting skill and solid art training of the court painter. The sheath is made of gilded silver inlaid with glass imitating rubies and sapphires, and the inlaid pieces of glass have been cut and polished like gems. This knife with its handle made of enamel-painted glass is extremely rare among the many such knives worn at the waist.

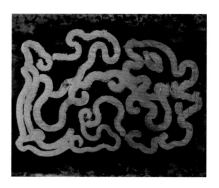

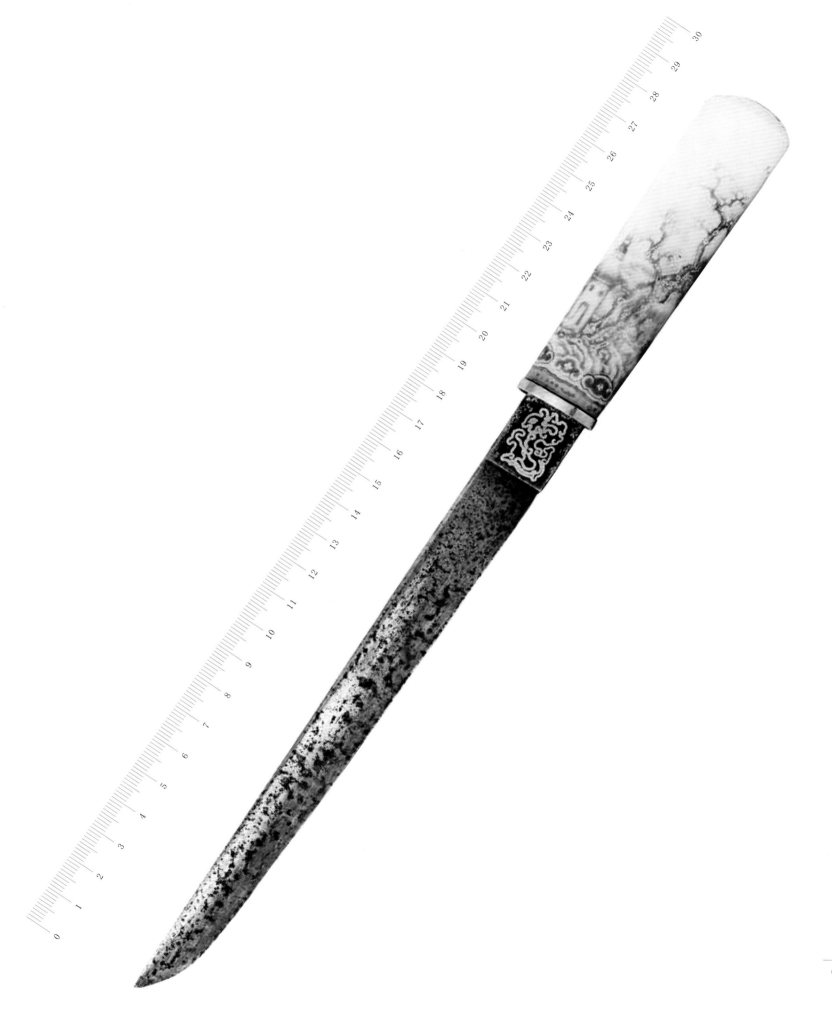

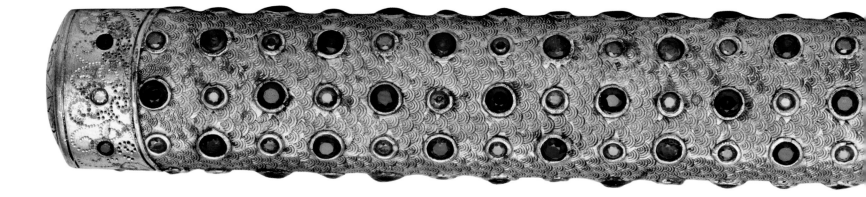

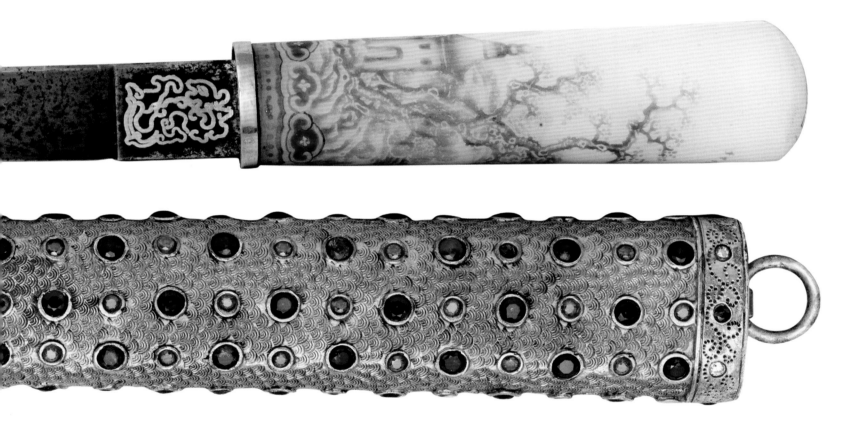

Opaque white glass snuff bottle with hornless-dragon design painted in enamel

Period: Qing
Inscription: Made in the Qianlong era
Dimensions: h. 39 mm, mouth outer diam. 15 mm, mouth inner diam. 8.5 mm

This snuff bottle is in the shape of an octagonal flat bottle, with a level bottom. The bottom is inscribed in regular script in blue glass *Qianlong nian zhi* ('Made in the Qianlong era'). The opaque-white glass base is painted with pink enamel. The front and back of the bottle are both convex, depicting a pair of one-footed dragons, one blue and one green, intertwined. These are encircled by a pattern of blue and coloured plant tendrils and flowers. The shape of the bottle is graceful and proportioned, the design is coherent and fresh, and the colours are harmonious. It is an exquisite piece from the glass factory at the palace workshops. Unfortunately, for one reason or another, this snuff bottle has been damaged, and the coloured enamel shows some imperfections.

Opaque white glass snuff bottle with all-over flowers painted in enamel

Period: Qing
Inscription: Guyue Xuan
Dimensions: h. 61 mm, mouth outer diam. 12.9 mm, mouth inner diam. 6.3 mm

This snuff bottle has a long, round belly and a rounded foot. The bottom is inscribed in blue glass *Guyue Xuan* ('Ancient Moon Pavilion'). The opaque-white glass is painted with coloured enamel. The body is covered in multi-coloured flowers, and the gaps in between filled with gold. The overall effect is of magnificence, embodying the court aesthetics of the Qianlong era.

Opaque white glass flat round snuff bottle with a ball-flower design painted in enamel

Period: Qing
Inscription: Guyue Xuan
Dimensions: h. 53.5 mm

This snuff bottle is flat and round in shape, with a level bottom and no foot. The bottom is inscribed in red glass *Guyue Xuan* ('Ancient Moon Pavilion'). The opaque-white glass is painted with coloured enamel, in a continuous ball-flower design. The ball flower was a new design feature of the Yongzheng reign, a noble adornment used by the emperor at the Qing palace. With its irregular layout and rich colours, the design conveys a unique and fresh aesthetic. The ball flowers of the Yongzheng and Qianlong eras are delicate, vivid and well spaced, giving an overall impression of scattering, vibrant colour and refinement. They bloom with a gorgeous and subtle beauty, quietly conveying such Chan (Zen) concepts as 'materiality and emptiness' and 'movement and stillness'. From the Daoguang era (1820–50) onwards, the ball-flower design became monotonous and lacked innovation.

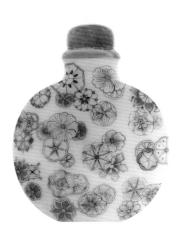

Opaque white glass snuff bottle with relief riches and good-fortune painted in enamel

Period: Qing
Inscription: Made in the Qianlong era
Dimensions: h. 51 mm, mouth outer diam. 15 mm, mouth inner diam. 8 mm

Opaque white glass snuff bottle with good-fortune and longevity pattern painted in enamel
Period: Qing
Inscription: Guyue Xuan
Dimensions: h. 52.6 mm

Opaque white glass snuff bottle with relief bamboo-and-stone bird-and-flower design painted in enamel

Period: Qing

Inscription: Guyue Xuan

Dimensions: h. 49.6 mm, mouth outer diam. 15.1 mm, mouth inner diam. 7.2 mm

Opaque white glass gourd-shaped snuff bottle with all-over flowers painted in enamel

Period: Qing
Inscription: Jingzhi
Dimensions: h. 32.7 mm

Opaque white glass snuff bottle with relief basket-and-flowers painted in enamel

Period: Qing
Inscription: Caihua Hall
Dimensions: h. 51 mm, mouth outer diam. 15 mm, mouth inner diam. 8 mm

This snuff bottle is in the shape of a flower basket, with a circular foot. The bottom is inscribed in red glass *Caihua Tang* ('Magnificent Hall'). The white glass is painted in coloured enamel. The lower half is carved and coloured to look like a bamboo basket, and on the upper half stems of flowers are depicted, such that the whole resembles a basket of flowers in bloom. This is an art that combines modelling, carving and painting.

The form of expression is refreshingly novel and unique. On porcelain, the *Caihua Tang* mark is relatively common, but much rarer on colour-enamelled glass.

Opaque white glass egg-shaped snuff bottle with multicoloured landscape-and-figure continuous scene painted in enamel

Period: Qing
Dimensions: h. 38 mm

This snuff bottle is egg-shaped, with a concave foot. On white glass a continuous landscape-and-figure scene is depicted. The bottle is dainty, exquisite and attractively smooth. The white glass base is as glossy as jade, the enamel painting beautifully delicate, and the composition elegantly intricate. This painting shows an autumn landscape. The distant mountains look like dark eyebrows, red leaves spray the branches, a stream is babbling, and a little bridge crosses the flowing water by a house. Within the house sits a scholar either enjoying tea or reading a book, a tranquil and leisurely scene. This painting has a lofty artistic conception and is of a high artistic quality. Moreover, to paint a continuous landscape-and-figure scene in such a small space is the greatest challenge for the craftsman. It is also the ultimate demand of the court aesthetic. This is an exquisite artefact of palace glass-base enamel painting.

Opaque white glass gold-ground snuff bottle with peony design painted in enamel

Period: Qing
Dimensions: h. 43 mm, mouth outer diam. 14 mm, mouth inner diam. 7.2 mm

Opaque white glass double snuff bottle with multicoloured stone-and-plant designs painted in enamel

Period: Qing
Inscription: Wanya Xuan
Dimensions: h. 42.5 mm

Opaque white glass lidded box with multicoloured *ruyi* design outlined in gold painted in enamel
Period: Qing
Dimensions: h. 26.5 mm

The incense box is a small container for incense. In classical times, the literati, in an appreciation for elegance, would burn incense in their studies and dining rooms. Since incense mostly came in pellets, cakes, natural wood, etc., the fragrance easily became volatile, and so the incense box came into use. In the studies of the literati, the attention focused on the incense box was not inferior to that paid to other objects related to reading and writing. This lidded box in opaque-white glass painted in coloured enamel and with *ruyi* ('as you desire') pattern traced in gold is an outstanding example of such incense boxes. The body is covered with intertwined tendrils and flowers, and the *ruyi* pattern on the lid stands out in relief. This design brings an elegance and grandeur to the box, imbuing it with an imperial flavour, and it represents a treasure among coloured enamels.

Opaque white glass snuff bottle with bird-and-flower and stone design painted in enamel

Period: Qing
Dimensions: h. 53.7 mm

Monochrome glass was one of the most important kinds of palace glass. The Qing court's colour requirements for glass far exceeded those of the European glass manufacturing industry at the time. Not only precious-stone colours, but also the hues of jade, jadeite, tourmaline, amber, coral, lapis lazuli, turquoise, realgar and similar substances were imitated. Colours associated with the Chinese literati's appreciation of the beauty of nature, such as 'the sky after a shower', lake green, watermelon juice, moonlight, chicken-fat yellow and lotus-root pink, were also created.

MONOCHROME GLASS

Transparent purple glass snuff bottle

Period: Qing Qianlong
Dimensions: h. 57 mm

This snuff bottle is in the shape of a vase, with a lip, a circular foot and no inscription. The surface shows signs of calcification, with the alkali-leaching to which early glass is prone visible, and it has marks of wear throughout. The transparent purple colour is very beautiful in the light – the only artefact of a similar colour is a water pot with a *Kangxi yuzhi* ('made at the order of the Kangxi emperor') in the Andrew K. F. Lee (Li Jingxu) collection shown in the exhibition catalogue *Elegance and Radiance: Grandeur in Qing Glass* (*Hongying yaohui*, 2000).

Transparent citrine-colour glass octagonal water holder

Period: Qing
Inscription: Made in the Yongzheng era
Dimensions: h. 46.3 mm

This water holder is in the shape of an octagonal droplet, with a slanting mouth and swelling belly, made in transparent citrine-colour glass throughout. The centre of the bottom is carved with a simple box, in which is inscribed in regular script *Yongzheng nianzhi* ('Made in the Yongzheng era') in two vertical columns. The water holder is made up of eight connected angular surfaces, both internally and externally – this is quite unlike the more common model of an angular outside and rounded inside. This shape greatly increases the difficulty of making the object. Moreover, the water holder is very hard to the touch, its walls are of uniform thickness, its lines graceful and smooth, its surfaces highly polished, and the imitation-citrine colour is refined and beautiful – the embodiment of Qing palace aesthetic taste. It is a fine example of Yongzheng-period (1723–35) glassware.

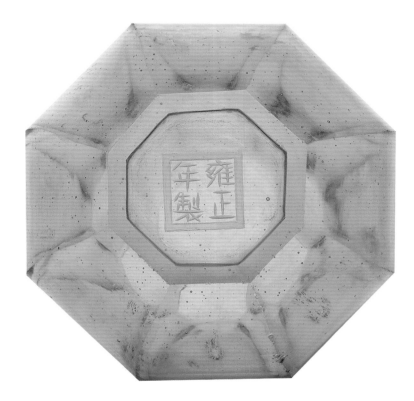

Songhua inkstone with Yongzheng inscription: Blue glass embedded-tourmaline inkstone box with relief one-legged dragon–phoenix design

Period: Qing
Inscription: Made in the Yongzheng era
Dimensions: l. 102 mm, w. 85 mm, h. 25 mm

Inkstones were relatively common objects at the palace, indispensable to the writing process in classical times. The Qing emperors greatly praised the Songhua inkstone. This particular Songhua inkstone, with a Yongzheng inscription, is composed of two co-occurring colours – yellow-ish and blue-ish. It is very rare, and a treasure among inkstones. The glass inkstone box custom-made for this inkstone is an even more superior item.

The box is divided into upper and lower parts, made of two kinds of blue glass. The lower part is in light-blue glass, and is embedded with what look like small translucent grains of crystal. This kind of glass has never been found on other objects. The upper part of the box is a thin dark-blue lid, carved with a stylized *kui* ('one-legged') dragon and phoenix pattern, which is inlaid with tourmaline in various colours – the carved design is extremely beautiful. This piece is unique in its glass carving with gemstones inlaid, and it represents the ultimate expression of the Yongzheng emperor's aesthetic. Extant glassware with inscriptions of the Yongzheng period is already rare, most of it being monochrome glass. This item with its inscription, carving and inlay is unmatched in Qing-period palace glass, and is a rare treasure.

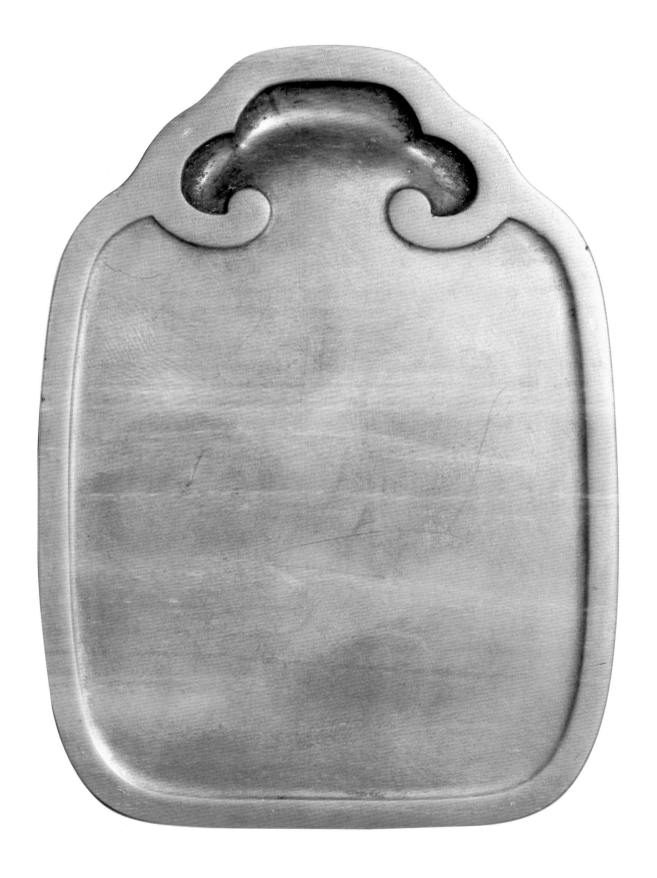

Transparent carmine-red glass fragrance box with chrysanthemum-petal pattern

Period: Qing
Dimensions: h. 43 mm

This lidded box is round in shape, with a circular foot and no inscription. Comprising a bottom part and a lid, the box is transparent and a carmine-red colour. With its chrysanthemum-petal design and small size, it could sit in the palm of the hand, just like a real chrysanthemum in full bloom. The Yongzheng emperor greatly admired the chrysanthemum flower, with a special liking for its shape, having various objects made in this form. Carmine red was also a favourite of the emperor. The natural combination of chrysanthemum and the red colour is incredibly beautiful. The box displays an unusual gracefulness of design, purity of colour and lustrous smoothness – moreover, it can be said to exemplify the aesthetic taste of Yongzheng. What is even rarer, however, is the flower-petal design of the bottom part and the lid, such that no matter in which orientation the lid is closed, the petals fit perfectly, reflecting the consummate quality and technique of court craftsmanship. Although this box has no inscription, it represents a typical example of the elegance and fine workmanship of the Yongzheng period.

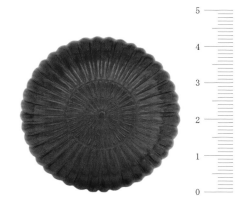

Sky-blue glass paperweight in the form of a rabbit

Period: Qing
Dimensions: h. 33.3 mm

The paperweight is a traditional object of the study, used to hold down paper when writing and painting. The most common are rectangular. Records show that the paperweight has a history of more than 1,500 years. The earliest were not fixed in shape. The origins of this object lie in the small bronze and jade items that the literati put on their desks to appreciate and handle. Because these inevitably had a certain weight, so they became used to hold down paper or to keep books in place. Gradually, over time, they developed into a recognized object of the study – the paperweight.

This animal-shaped paperweight is rare in glassware. Its unsullied, tasteful sky-blue colour, richly tactile quality, little red eyes, and attractive rabbit modelling, in fact represent unusual craftsmanship for objects of the study. Good paperweights have both practical and artistic features. Especially in studies that are fastidiously furnished, the paperweight embodies a finishing touch reflecting the owner's hobbies and tastes. This rabbit-shaped paperweight is of peerless brilliance and extremely precious.

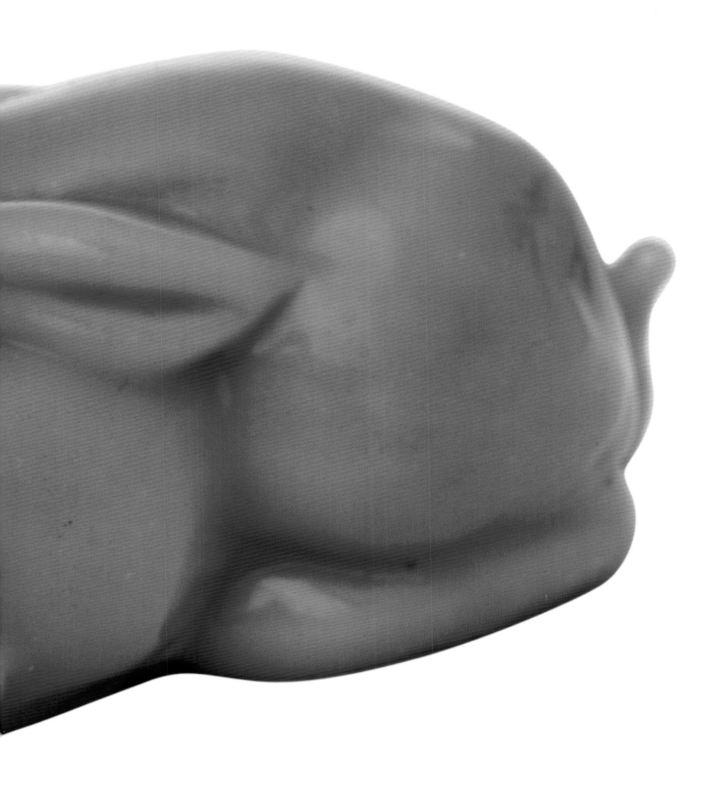

Transparent imitation-gemstone red glass plum-blossom shaped lidded box with yin-yang design

Period: Qing
Inscription: Made in the Qianlong era
Dimensions: h. 56.7 mm

This box is shaped like a six-petal blossom, and is comprised of bottom part and lid. It has a composite mouth and a rounded foot. The body is transparent imitation-gemstone red throughout, the centre of the lid is carved with a Taiji (yin-yang) design, and there are six petals around it, like a delicate, red blossom. The bottom is inscribed in intaglio in regular script *Qianlong nian zhi* ('Made in the Qianlong era') in two vertical columns. This lidded box is graceful and elegant in appearance, the colour is bold, and the material is pure – without a single bubble. It is an outstanding masterpiece of early Qianlong (1735–96) glass.

Transparent imitation-amber glass plum-blossom shaped lidded box

Period: Qing Qianlong
Dimensions: h. 32.7 mm

This box is shaped like a five-petal plum blossom, and is comprised of bottom part and lid. It has a composite mouth and a rounded foot. The body is transparent imitation-amber colour throughout, the surface is lustrous, and from above it looks like a translucent blooming plum blossom. This lidded box is graceful and elegant in appearance, the colour is true, and the material is pure. Although it has no inscription, it is an unusually fine glass product of the Qianlong period.

Transparent green glass plum-blossom shaped lidded box with yin-yang design
Period: Qing Qianlong
Dimensions: h. 32.7 mm

This box is shaped like a six-petal blossom, and is comprised of bottom part and lid. It has a composite mouth and a rounded foot. The body is transparent jade-green throughout, the centre of the lid is carved with a Taiji (yin-yang) design, and there are six petals around it, like a blooming jade-green plum blossom.

Transparent imitation-gemstone red glass bundle-shaped water holder with tied-rope pattern

Period: Qing
Dimensions: h. 45.4 mm

This water holder is in the shape of a natural-looking bag, with no foot, a swelling belly and slightly gathered mouth. Near the mouth, a rope appears to run through the bag, with knots to the left and right sides falling naturally, as if the opening could be readily extended. There is no inscription. This style is modelled exactly on porcelain of the Yongzheng period. Although there is no inscription, the water holder's crystal-clear body, without a single bubble, and ruby-like tactile quality, along with its elegant and noble shape, reveal it as possessing the superior aesthetic quality of Yongzheng-period objects of the study.

Transparent imitation-gemstone red glass *ruyi* lidded box

Period: Qing
Dimensions: l. 63 mm, w. 43 mm, h. 27 mm

This box has a *ruyi* ('as you desire') shape, and is comprised of bottom part and lid. It has a composite mouth and a rounded foot. The body is transparent and a gemstone-red colour throughout. The glass was smelted with gold and minerals as colouring agents. Red glass occupied a large part of the glassware produced during the Qianlong era. A great amount was produced in this pure and gorgeous colour, indicating that the craftsmen of the time had mastered its formula and smelting technology.

This lidded box is delicate and exquisite, the *ruyi* design shows great ingenuity, and the colour is pure, as if it were made of real ruby. Although there is no inscription, it can be recognized as a fine example of monochrome Qianlong-era glass.

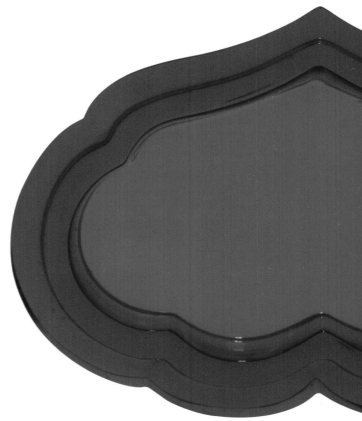

Transparent carmine-red glass lidded box with sunflower pattern

Period: Qing
Dimensions: h. 42.2 mm

This box is round in shape, and is comprised of bottom part and lid. It has a composite mouth and a circular foot. The body is transparent and a carmine-red colour throughout, perfectly round and finely polished, evincing purity and gorgeousness. The sunflower design is quite brilliant – this box is outstanding among incense objects of the study.

Transparent lake-water green glass snuff bottle with cross-shaped ground edges

Period: Qing
Inscription: Made in the Qianlong era
Dimensions: h. 39.5 mm

Transparent gemstone-blue glass ground-edge shaped snuff bottle

Period: Qing
Inscription: Made in the Qianlong era
Dimensions: h. 40.4 mm, mouth outer diam. 13.5 mm, mouth inner diam. 7.7 mm

This snuff bottle is octagonal in shape, with a straight neck, round mouth and flat bottom. The body is gemstone-blue transparent glass throughout. The bottom is inscribed in intaglio in regular script *Qianlong nian zhi* ('Made in the Qianlong era'). The bottle is delicate and simple – both front and back are cut like a diamond, with convex panels. It is witness to a fusion of Western and Eastern cultures.

Transparent sea-water blue glass double snuff bottle
Period: Qing
Dimensions: h. 44.8 mm

This double snuff bottle is in the shape of two composite flat bottles, with straight necks and concave feet, and the body is sea-blue throughout. The surface is plain and pattern-less, the colour bright and gorgeous, and the bottle is crystal clear. It is extremely rare in monochrome glass.

Gold-flecked green glass double-layer snuff bottle

Period: Qing
Inscription: Made in the Qianlong era
Dimensions: h. 46.3 mm

This snuff bottle is in the shape of a vase, with a straight mouth, broad shoulders, and a circular foot. The body is opaque green glass throughout, with glittering gold flecks of various sizes. Within the circular foot is inscribed in intaglio in regular script *Qianlong nian zhi* ('Made in the Qianlong era'). Few green glass gold-flecked snuff bottles have survived, and, as a unique kind of the Qianlong-period glassware, they are very valuable.

Blue glass gold-flecked incense burner with bridge handles

Period: Qing
Dimensions: h. 80 mm

The incense burner is an indispensable item in Chinese religion, folk custom and sacrificial culture, and is also an essential tool for incense. The prototype of the three-legged burner can be traced back to the bronzes of the Shang and Zhou periods (2nd to 1st millennium BCE). The Qing palace used a variety of materials, including glass, to make them.

This incense burner is round in shape, with a swelling belly, flared mouth, bridge handles, and three breast-shaped feet. The body is opaque blue glass throughout, with glittering gold flecks. Gold-flecked glass is a precious kind of glass, with a manufacture technique that originated in Europe. In the sixth year of Qianlong, the glass factory at the Qing palace successfully produced gold-flecked glass under the guidance of Western missionaries. The manufacturing method is different to that for other kinds of glass. First, the raw materials are melted in a crucible to create blocks, and then these are ground as in the method for cutting and polishing jade to create objects. Gold-flecked glass was produced only under Qianlong, and it is rare; the blue gold-flecked variety is particularly difficult to trace, and is recorded merely in the Qing palace workshop records. There are only forty or more pieces of gold-flecked glass in the Palace Museum, Beijing, all of which are brown gold-flecked glass. This is the only example of blue gold-flecked glass currently known to be extant, and extremely valuable.

Transparent wine-yellow glass two-handled incense burner
Period: Qing
Dimensions: h. 35 mm

Lemon-yellow glass incense burner with bridge handles
Period: Qing
Dimensions: h. 41 mm

Transparent wine-yellow glass incense burner with bridge handles

Period: Qing
Dimensions: h. 54.5 mm

Transparent imitation-gemstone red glass incense burner with halberd handles

Period: Qing
Dimensions: h. 40.4 mm

Transparent carmine-red glass polygonal drum-shaped water holder
Period: Qing
Dimensions: h. 36.8 mm

This water holder is in the shape of a drum, with a swelling belly, pulled-in mouth and circular foot. The surface of the object is multi-edged, to look like a cut gem, and it is a transparent carmine red throughout. The holder is delicate and exquisite, the glass crystal-clear, and the carmine-red colour pure and gorgeous. The craft of gem-cutting makes the object seem even more elegant and magnificent.

Transparent grape-purple glass lidded box

Period: Qing
Inscription: Made in the Qianlong era
Dimensions: h. 51.7 mm

This lidded box is round in shape, comprised of bottom part and lid. It has a composite mouth and a circular foot. The body is a transparent grape-purple colour throughout. The bottom is inscribed in intaglio traced in gold in regular script *Qianlong nian zhi* ('Made in the Qianlong era') in two vertical columns.

The box is plain and pattern-less, relying entirely on the purity of the glass and the clarity of the colour in its appeal, reflecting the superb quality of glass production under Qianlong – it is representative of Qianlong glass products.

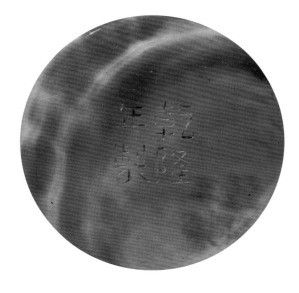

Imitation lapis-lazuli water holder with Eight-Trigram pattern

Period: Qing
Inscription: Made in the Qianlong era
Dimensions: h. 29.4 mm

This water holder is flat and round in shape, with a swelling belly, pulled-in mouth and circular foot. This belly is carved in high relief with an Eight Trigram pattern, and it is an opaque lapis-lazuli blue throughout. The bottom is inscribed in intaglio in regular script *Qianlong nian zhi* ('Made in the Qianlong era') in two vertical columns. Carved glass is an important kind of glass manufacture of the Qianlong period. It is similar to cut jade, and this water holder was carved using the jade cutting and polishing method.

Transparent imitation-gemstone blue glass water pot with chrysanthemum-petal pattern

Period: Qing
Inscription: Made in the Qianlong era
Dimensions: h. 62.7 mm

This water holder is round in shape, with a swelling belly, pulled-in mouth and circular foot. The belly is carved with a chrysanthemum-petal pattern, and it is a transparent gemstone blue throughout. The bottom is inscribed in intaglio in regular script *Qianlong nian zhi* ('Made in the Qianlong era') in two vertical columns. The water holder is large and regular in shape. The gemstone-blue colour is pure and translucent, and the glass-carving craft adds gives the item a nobility and gorgeousness. It is a precious object of the study.

Transparent boxwood-green glass eight-segment shaped water holder with flower mouth

Period: Qing
Dimensions: h. 24.4 mm

This water holder has a flat and round flower-petal shape, with a pulled-in mouth and circular foot. It is a translucent boxwood green throughout. In traditional times, people had a talent for observing and expressing the beauty of nature, and integrating these colours into their lives in all sorts of contexts. The boxwood green is the colour of spring leaves that have just come out, fresh and tender, a relatively rare colour for glass items. The surface of the water holder is highly polished, and the octagonal petal shape exquisitely aesthetic. The modelling and decoration are ingeniously combined, reflecting innovative craftsmanship, and this is a handsome object of the study.

Transparent pink glass *shishi ruyi* lidded box

Period: Qing Qianlong
Dimensions: h. 26.4 mm

This lidded box is the shape of an embellished square, and comprised of a bottom part and lid. It has a composite mouth and circular foot, and is transparent pink throughout. The four corners have *ruyi* ('as you desire') patterns in high relief. The box is finely carved, and possesses a natural elegance. The pink tone is unusual, glittering and translucent, and achingly delicate. The box is an outstanding work of Qianlong-period glassware.

Imitation-turquoise green mountain-shaped brush rest

Period: Qing
Inscription: Made in the Qianlong era
Dimensions: h. 150 mm

The brush rest is one of the commonly used items in the traditional Chinese study. This glass brush rest is modelled on Qing-period porcelain brush rests, in a natural free-form mountain shape. It is punctuated with holes of different sizes, with something of the charm of travertine, rich in innate interest. The imitation-turquoise colour is not uniform, but it has exceptional charm, like a natural texture. The bottom is inscribed in intaglio in regular script *Qianlong nian zhi* ('Made in the Qianlong era'). It is a very rare elegant object of the study.

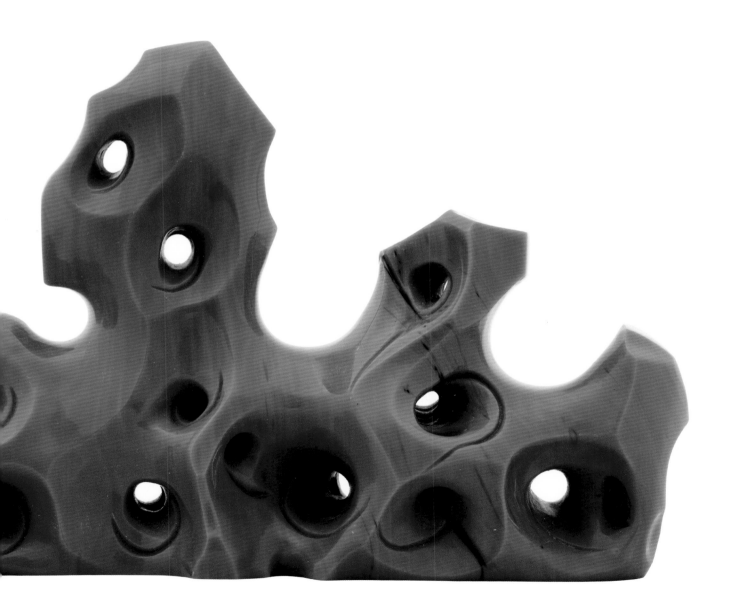

Feng-character inkstone with Qianlong imperial inscription: Transparent imitation-gemstone blue glass inkstone box

Period: Qing
Dimensions: l. 130 mm, w. 125 mm, h. 40 mm

This inkstone is in the shape of the character *feng* meaning 'wind'. The top is plain, with a crescent-shaped well hollowed out; the bottom is flat, with a poem in the Qianlong emperor's regular script inscribed in intaglio traced in gold. Around the edge is engraved *fang Song tiancheng fengzi yan* ('imitation-Song style naturally-formed feng-character inkstone').

The material of which the inkstone is made is solid, dense and fine, and the shape is simple and elegant. It is beautifully carved – a typically fine piece of the Qianlong court, replete with a gemstone-blue inkstone box. The inkstone box is a lidded box with a composite mouth, lustrously smooth and highly transparent. Inkstones at the palace were accompanied by various kinds of inkstone box, but boxes made of glass are extremely rare.

春之德風大塊噫氣施蟲

諧聲於凡制字告則為雨

潤物斯濟石星相琴行若

郪置豈惟天成亦有人事

揆而議之既純且悴

足敦隆御銘

Chicken-fat yellow long-necked vase with hunting-scene panel and Manchu-Chinese imperial inscription

Period: Qing
Inscription: Made in the Qianlong era
Dimensions: h. 253 mm

This vase was formed using a blowing technique, and has a swelling belly, long neck, and circular foot. It is chicken-fat yellow throughout, with two panels, one on either side of the belly. One panel shows a hunting scene in intaglio; the other is inscribed in Manchu. The two remaining sides do not have panels. On one is written in the emperor's calligraphic style Du Fu's poem *Xiaozhi* ('Winter Solstice'); on the other is the interpretation of the poem. On the bottom of the circular foot is inscribed in intaglio in regular script *Qianlong nian zhi* ('Made in the Qianlong era') in two vertical columns. Yellow has always been the colour used exclusively by the emperor, symbolizing imperial power. The vase is well-proportioned, smooth and lustrous, and the colour resembles the yellow of chicken fat. Inclusion of both Manchu and Chinese script is rare. It is a masterpiece of the Qianlong period.

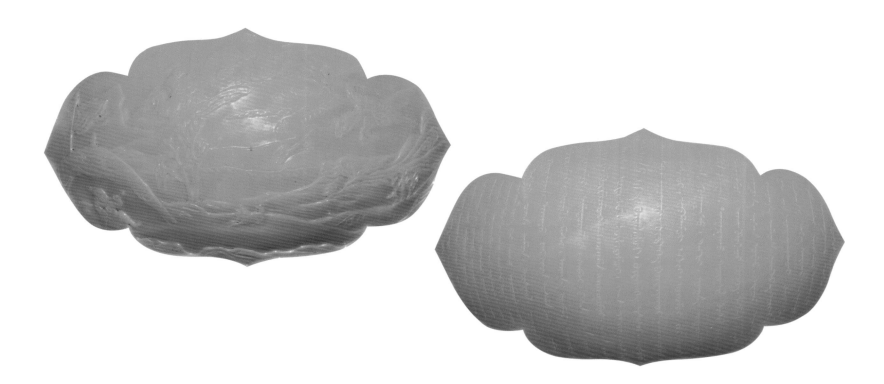

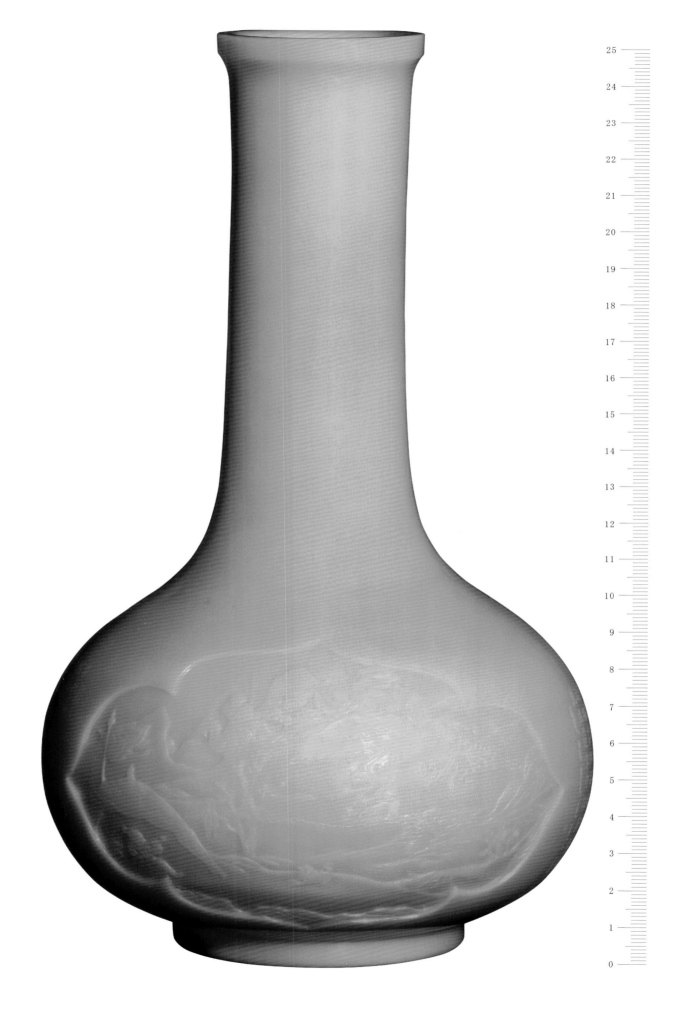

25
24
23
22
21
20
19
18
17
16
15
14
13
12
11
10
9
8
7
6
5
4
3
2
1
0

Imitation-coral red double-fish *zun* vessel

Period: Qing
Inscription: Made in the Qianlong era
Dimensions: h. 212 mm

This *zun* vessel is in the shape of two conjoined fish, with one side of the bodies of each of the fish set opposite each other, quite symmetrically. The fish-*zun* is lifelike – the mouths of the fish are the vessel's mouth, the eyes protrude, and the bodies swell slightly. A pair of dorsal fins are located opposite each other, and four pairs of belly fins are inter-connected. The fishtails are slightly flared, and the bottom of the fish-*zun* is encircled by a water-ripple pattern, as if the two fish were standing on the waves. The double-fish (*yu*) implies 'successive years of abundance (*yu* – a homonym), harmony and happiness'. Traditionally, people also regarded the fish as a symbol of yin and yang: 'The fish jumps into the depths, and passes through yin and yang.' The heart of the Taiji design comprises two yin-and-yang fish conjoined. The form of the double fish as one fits with this concept of the yin-and-yang fish.

This double-fish *zun* is large, lifelike and elegant, and the coral-red colour is vivid. The outer part of the bottom is inscribed in intaglio in seal script *Qianlong nian zhi* ('Made in the Qianlong era') in two vertical columns. It is a rare masterpiece of the Qianlong period.

Transparent glass gourd-shaped vase

Period: Qing
Inscription: Made in the Qianlong era
Dimensions: h. 184.5 mm

This vase is in the shape of a gourd, with a straight mouth, accentuated waist and circular foot. It is transparent and colourless glass throughout. The bottom is inscribed in intaglio in regular script *Qianlong nian zhi* ('Made in the Qianlong era') in two vertical columns. Owing to its distinctive shape and other characteristics, the gourd has many positive associations. The shape of the gourd is like the character *ji*, meaning 'auspicious'. The word for 'gourd' is *hulu* sounding a little like *fulu*, implying 'riches and longevity', increasing the affection felt for the object. The gourd is composed of circles, which symbolize harmony and contentment. Furthermore, because gourd vines continue unbroken, and they bear seeds and proliferate, the gourd is regarded as a lucky charm for those hoping for offspring.

Transparent blue glass Hall of Spiritual Cultivation imperial seal with auspicious-beast knob

Period: Qing Qianlong
Inscription: Yangxing Dian
Dimensions: h. 36.5 mm, l. 32 mm

The Hall of Spiritual Cultivation (Yangxing Dian) is located within the Gate of Spiritual Cultivation (Yangxing Men) at the back of the Palace of Tranquil Longevity (Ningshou Gong) in the Forbidden City, Beijing. It is one of the main buildings of the residential rear quarter of the Palace of Tranquil Longevity. It was built in the thirty-seventh year of the Qianlong reign (1772), modelled the Hall of Mental Cultivation (Yangxin Dian) in the inner court, but with slightly smaller proportions and a distinctive layout. This Hall of Spiritual Cultivation seal with its *suoni* beast knob was the palace imperial seal used by the Qianlong emperor when he was living in the Hall of Spiritual Cultivation after his abdication in favour of his son. The knob is sculpted in the round as a *suoni*, rather like a lion, lifting its head from the stamping pad, with the air of a leader of beasts, exquisitely carved, and with strong three-dimensionality. The stamp consists of three characters *Yangxing Dian* carved in relief in seal script. Because the seal is made of imported glass, it is dense and hard, and not easily carved. Therefore, it was carved employing special engraving techniques used for the jade items produced at the Hall of Mental Cultivation palace workshops, and conveys a sturdy compactness and solidity. The *suoni* knob is unique to the Qing palace, used exclusively by the inner court, and it is an extremely high-grade imperial seal knob. This seal is clearly of superior form and noble character, reflecting a self-awareness on the part of the emperors of the period, transporting the viewer to a perfect and lofty physical and mental state, with the dazzling radiance of an imperial object.

Transparent lake-green glass ritual implement

Period: Qing
Dimensions: h. 101.7 mm

This glass vajra ritual implement is a lake-green colour, and the material is pure. It was carved employing special engraving techniques used for the jade items produced at the palace workshops. It is not only stately, but also transparent as water. Buddhists regard cultivating 'body and soul to become like coloured glass' as the highest state. The palace used glass items as ritual implements, embodying the solemnity and sacredness of imperial Buddhist devotion.

Conch shell inset with gemstone-blue glass presented at the Baoxiang Changxin Hall in the fifth year of Qianlong

Period: Qing
Inscription: Fifth Year of Qianlong
Dimensions: l. 130.8 mm, w. (h.) 78.2 mm

This conch shell is right-handed, and the outside is white, plain and delicate. A natural form, it is inlaid with gemstone-blue glass at its tip, and inscribed *Baoxiang Changxin Dian Qianlong wu nian gonggong* 'presented at the Baoxiang Changxin Hall in the fifth year of Qianlong' along its edge. The Baoxiang Changxin Hall is a courtyard in the Puren Temple at the Chengde Mountain Resort. This was the imperial temple erected by the Kangxi emperor to accommodate public officials on the occasion of sixtieth birthday. Over the main entrance to the hall hangs a horizontal tablet inscribed in Kangxi's calligraphy *Baoxiang Changxin*. The conch is smooth, and of medium size. The gemstone-blue glass inlay increases its rarity. The inscription shows that this object is a rare treasure from an imperial temple.

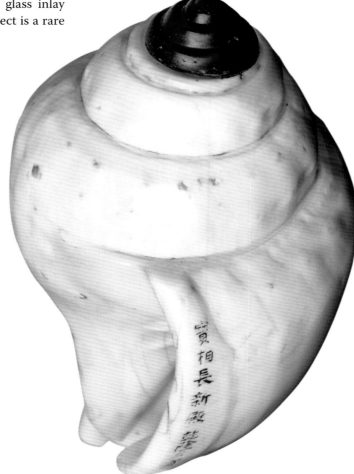

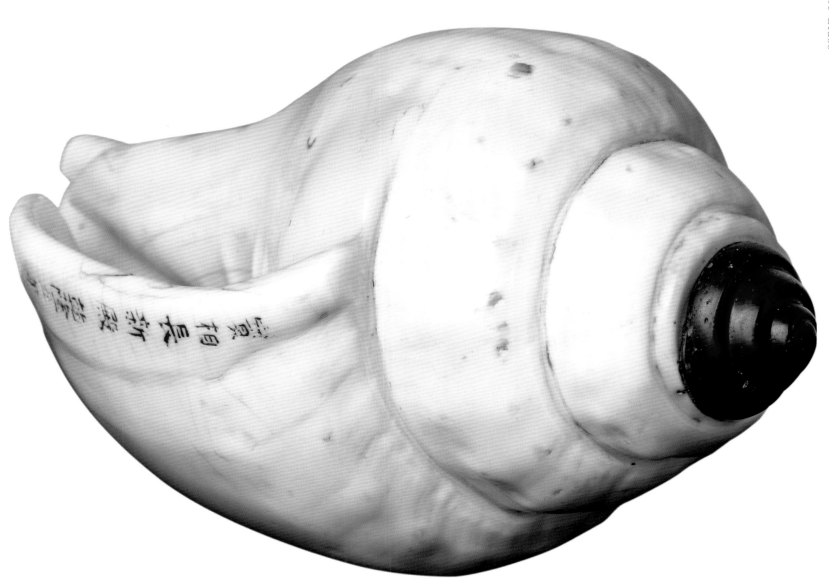

Coffee-coloured gold-flecked glass ritual implement

Period: Qing
Dimensions: l. 101.4 mm

This gold-flecked glass object represents a special kind of glassware. It was produced only in the time of Qianlong, and simply disappeared afterwards. Under the light, the gold-flecked glass twinkles seductively, like countless sparkling small gems, assuming a gorgeous sensuality. Gold-flecked glass vajra ritual implements are even more unusual, so this item is very rare.

Opaque white glass oval incensor

Period: Qing Yongzheng
Dimensions: h. 30.7 mm

This incense burner is oval in shape, with a swelling belly, slightly retracted mouth, and circular foot. It is opaque white throughout. The original lid is of openwork red sandalwood, set with a purple tourmaline at the top.

The incense burner is a jade-like white colour throughout, pure and smooth. It looks almost slippery, and pleasingly clean, an entirely elegant object of the study. In the Yongzheng and Qianlong periods, artistic style in glassware was very similar, characterized by fine craftsmanship and a certain imperial magnificence. In the first two decades of the Qianlong period, it reached an unprecedented peak. Glass has always prevailed by means of its pure and brilliant colours. When it occurs in pure white, it may fall short. This incense burner is as pale as lard, and as soft to the touch as a baby's skin. The shape is simple and elegant, with no need of embellishment. Just one touch further would be too much, and one touch less make the piece seem lacking. It reaches the highest level of taste and aesthetics. The uniqueness of this aesthetic and taste is surely an indication of Yongzheng. The burner has no inscription, and is almost certainly a work of the Yongzheng period.

Transparent imitation-gemstone blue glass handled cup

Period: Qing
Dimensions: h. 30.1 mm

The handled cup is a traditional drinking vessel. According to historical records, it first appeared in the Warring States period (5th century to 221 BCE). It was used for drinking wine or simmering broth, and was mostly made in wood and painted, but also in jade, gilded bronze, or other materials. The ancient form of this glass cup represents continuity with traditional Chinese culture.

The cup is oval in shape, with a pair of curved handles on each of the long sides and a round foot. It is a transparent gemstone-blue colour throughout, with an elegant and noble quality, representing the highest pursuit of traditional court aesthetics.

Transparent imitation-gemstone red glass snuff bottle with dragon design

Period: Qing
Dimensions: h. 50 mm, mouth outer diam. 14 mm, mouth inner diam. 7.7 mm

Transparent pink glass snuff bottle with ancient pattern
Period: Qing
Dimensions: h. 63.5 mm, mouth outer diam. 14 mm, mouth inner diam. 7.7 mm

Transparent imitation-gemstone red glass moon-vase shaped snuff bottle

Period: Qing
Inscription: Jiazi
Dimensions: h. 46.3 mm

Transparent carmine-red glass snuff bottle with rope pattern
Period: Qing
Dimensions: h. 57.9 mm, mouth outer diam. 19.5 mm, mouth inner diam.
12.2 mm

Imitation-realgar glass snuff bottle
Period: Qing
Dimensions: h. 65.3 mm

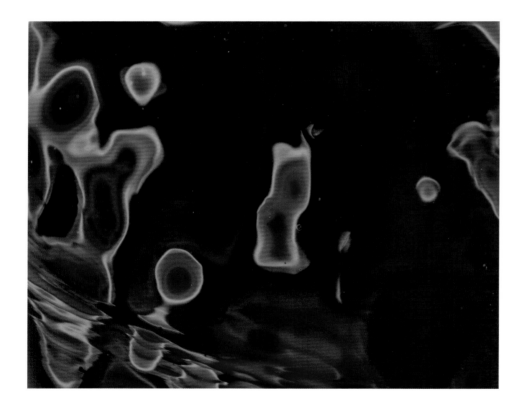

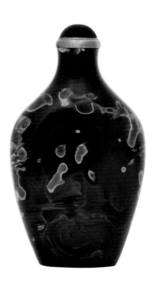

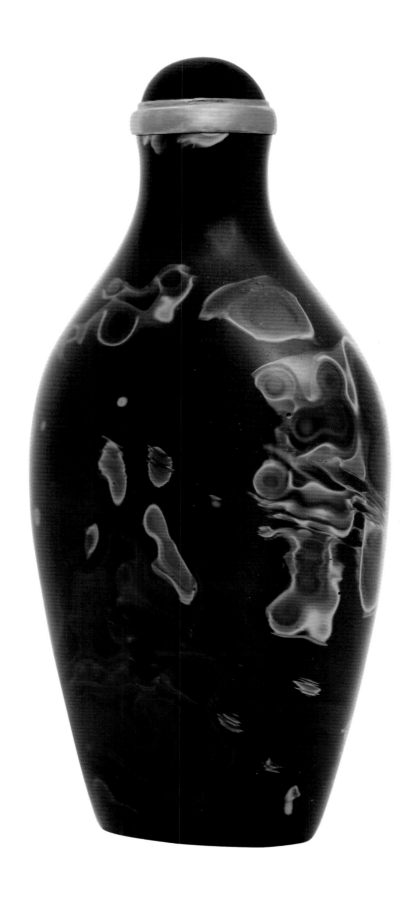

Transparent carmine-red glass flower-petal shaped snuff bottle
Period: Qing
Dimensions: h. 45.2 mm

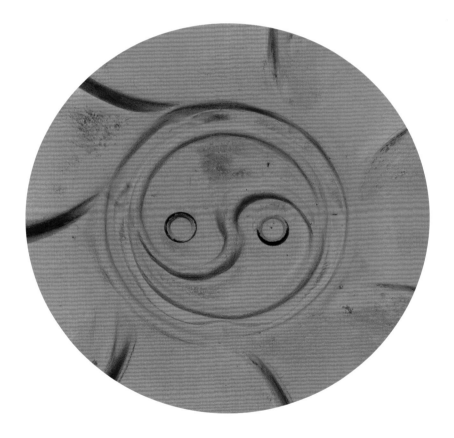

Lotus-root pink glass flower-petal shaped snuff bottle with ancient pattern

Period: Qing
Dimensions: h. 55.1 mm, mouth outer diam. 14.7 mm, mouth inner diam. 5.2 mm

This snuff bottle is in the shape of a flat bottle, with a rope-patterned mouth and a circular foot. It is transparent lotus-root pink glass throughout, and both sides are carved with a double-loop rope pattern. The colour of bottle is fresh and elegant, and the rope pattern is carved exquisitely and realistically, reflecting the superb glass modelling technology of the Qing palace glass factory.

Imitation-turquoise glass snuff bottle with chrysanthemum-and-stone design

Period: Qing
Dimensions: h. 48.7 mm, mouth outer diam. 15.1 mm, mouth inner diam. 7.8 mm

This snuff bottle is in the shape of a flat bottle, with a straight mouth, swelling belly and circular foot. It depicts stones and chrysanthemums in high relief, and is an opaque turquoise-green colour throughout.

Among the glass items created at the Qing palace, there are not many works decorated in relief, and all are finely carved, highly polished and exquisite. This is one of those pieces.

Lemon-yellow glass snuff bottle with three-dimensional infant-playing design

Period: Qing
Dimensions: h. 63 mm, mouth outer diam. 13 mm, mouth inner diam. 8 mm

This snuff bottle is in the shape of a flat bottle, and has a three-dimensional carving of an infant to one side. It is an opaque lemon-yellow colour throughout. This kind of three-dimensional carving of an infant playing is more common in porcelain, and is rare in glass. This item was created using a jade-carving technique and is of consummate workmanship. It is a fine glassware work of art.

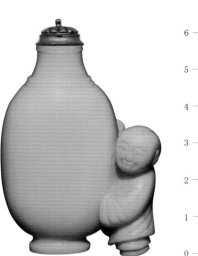

Transparent imitation-citrine glass egg-shaped snuff bottle
Period: Qing
Dimensions: h. 45.8 mm, neck 5.2 mm

This snuff bottle is egg-shaped, with a concave foot. It is a citrine colour throughout. It has an irregular wave pattern. Although this represents a small flaw, the inadvertent effect is to add an unexpected beauty to the object.

Transparent lotus-root pink glass handbell zun-shaped snuff bottle
Period: Qing
Dimensions: h. 46.1 mm

Transparent imitation-gemstone red glass moon-vase shaped snuff bottle with Eight-Trigram pattern

Period: Qing
Dimensions: h. 58.1 mm, mouth outer diam. 14 mm, mouth inner diam. 7.9 mm

Transparent imitation-citrine glass pomegranate *zun* water holder

Period: Qing

Dimensions: h. 57.5 mm

Transparent carmine-red glass mirror with swirl pattern

Period: Qing
Dimensions: h. 70.4 mm

This swirl-pattern mirror is round in shape, with a smooth, un-patterned hidden face, and a swirl pattern on top. It is a transparent carmine-red colour throughout. Swirl-pattern mirrors were a kind of Tang-period (618–907 CE) bronze mirror. This one is made of glass, and cannot be used as a mirror, making it a pseudo-classical amusement piece. The mirror is magnificent and gorgeous, the material pure, and the shape unusual for glassware. It represents a rare Qing court appreciation piece.

Transparent purple glass gourd-shaped brush rinsing bowl

Period: Qing
Inscription: Made in the Qianlong era
Dimensions: h. 40 mm, neck 13 mm

This brush-rinsing bowl is in the shape of a gourd, with a stalk at the tip, and is both natural-looking and charming. The upper part is narrow and the lower part broad, and it has an accentuated waist and a round foot. It is a transparent purple colour throughout. The bottom is inscribed in intaglio in regular script *Qianlong nian zhi* ('Made in the Qianlong era') in two vertical columns.

The gourd shape was a favourite at the court. This rinsing bowl is large, modelled stably and distinctively, with a glossy shine, and an understated restraint. It represented the final touch to the desk in the imperial study.

Opaque white glass peach-shaped snuff dish
Period: Qing
Inscription: Bing
Dimensions: h. 38.4 mm

Small imitation lapis-lazuli blue glass gourd-shaped brush dipper

Period: Qing
Dimensions: l. 57.3 mm

This brush dipper is in the shape of a gourd, with a stalk at the tip, a pontil mark at one end, and a flat bottom. It is an opaque lapis-lazuli blue colour throughout. The dipper is bright and colourful, and delicately wrought. Its small size suggests it was used by court women for painting their eyebrows. From this tiny object, we catch a glimpse of the palace women's privileged life spent making up and adorning themselves in front of a mirror.

Boxwood-green glass fragrance box with *ruyi* cloud pattern
Period: Qing
Dimensions: h. 25.4 mm

This lidded box is oval in shape, and comprised of bottom part and lid. It has a composite mouth and a rounded foot. It is a boxwood green colour throughout. The boxwood green is adorably fresh and tender, a relatively rare colour for glass items. The delicate and exquisite modelling, combined with the *ruyi* ('as you desire') auspicious ornamentation, the colour, workmanship and form all equate to a kind of perfection in glass.

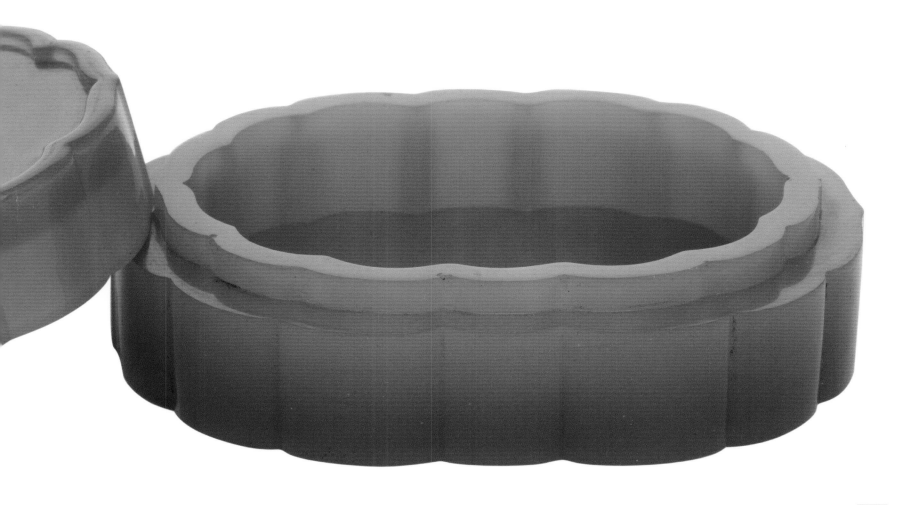

Purple glass aubergine-style ornament

Period: Qing
Dimensions: h. 170 mm

This aubergine ornament was made by blowing glass into a mould, and is dark purple throughout, with a green transparent-glass stalk at one end. It is very realistic. Glass items made in imitation of living objects are relatively rare.

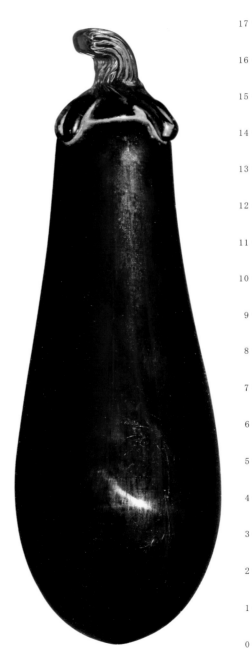

Transparent gemstone-blue snuff bottle with cross-shaped ground edges

Period: Qing
Inscription: Made in the Qianlong era
Dimensions: h. 39.8 mm

Transparent imitation-amber glass ground-edge shaped flower holder

Period: Qing Qianlong
Dimensions: h. 132.6 mm

This flower holder is cut in an angular shape, with a straight mouth, swelling belly, taller upper part and shorter lower part, and a flat bottom. It is a transparent amber colour throughout. The material is pure and extremely transparent. The ground geometric design feels modern in style and has a three-dimensional effect. This is a masterpiece of the Qianlong period. After the Qianlong period glass grinding technology went into decline.

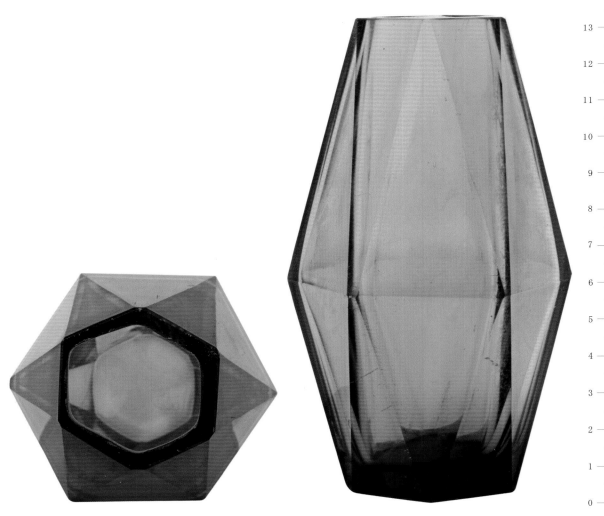

Transparent red glass olive vase

Period: Qing
Inscription: Made in the Qianlong era
Dimensions: h. 184 mm (including base)

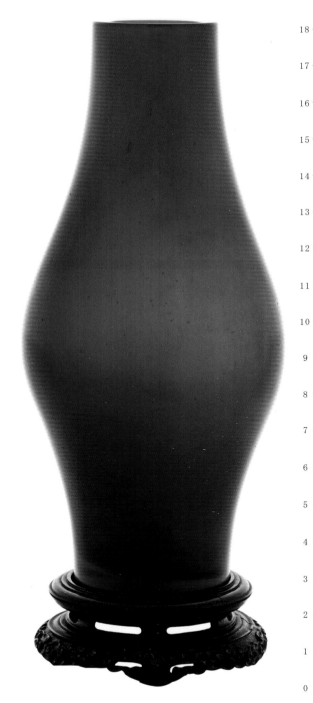

Small imitation-realgar glass cup

Period: Qing
Inscription: Made in the Qianlong era
Dimensions: h. 35.7 mm

This small cup is delicate, with a full shape, open mouth, shallow belly and concave foot. It is an opaque realgar colour throughout. The bottom is inscribed in intaglio in regular script *Qianlong nian zhi* ('Made in the Qianlong era') in two vertical columns.

The cup has thin walls, and is hard to the touch. The effect is dignified and neat, and typical of small cups of the Qianlong period. The shape of the concave foot cup originates in porcelain, again reflecting a combination of tradition and innovation.

Small semi-transparent pink glass cup

Period: Qing
Inscription: Made in the Jiaqing era
Dimensions: h. 33.4 mm

This small cup has an open mouth, shallow belly, and concave foot. It is translucent pink throughout. The bottom is inscribed in intaglio in regular script *Jiaqing nian zhi* ('Made in the Jiaqing era') in two vertical columns.

This cup has a distinctive colour and is full in shape, but displays small changes compared with the Qianlong period. It is less beautiful, and the walls are slightly thicker. Despite these changes, it is still a fine work of the Jiaqing era (1796–1820). Jiaqing items with inscriptions are especially rare. There are only seven such pieces in the Palace Museum, Beijing, so this cup is very valuable.

Transparent imitation-gemstone red glass flower-petal shaped brush-rinsing bowl

Period: Qing
Dimensions: h. 27.9 mm

This brush-rinsing bowl is round in shape, with a flared flower mouth, swelling belly, slightly restrained bottom, and circular foot. It is a pure gemstone-red colour throughout. The bowl is carved with a lotus petal design on its outer surface, and is beautifully modelled, hard to the touch, with not a single bubble, lustrous and transparent. The gemstone red is grand and elegant, one of the representative colours of glass cold-processing technology.

Transparent imitation-gemstone blue glass crabapple-cluster shaped brush-rinsing bowl
Period: Qing
Dimensions: h. 31.4mm

LIST OF ILLUSTRATIONS

MONOCHROME GLASS

VISUAL INDEX

page 58

page 60

page 62

page 64

page 70

page 72

page 74

page 76

page 78

page 80

page 84

page 86

page 88

page 90

page 92

page 93

page 96

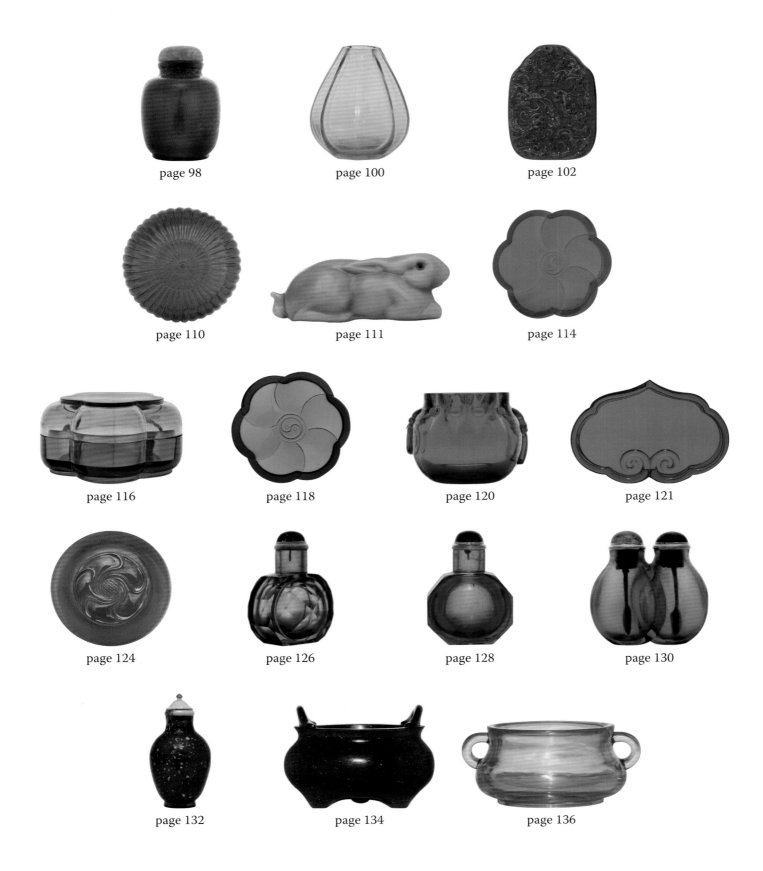

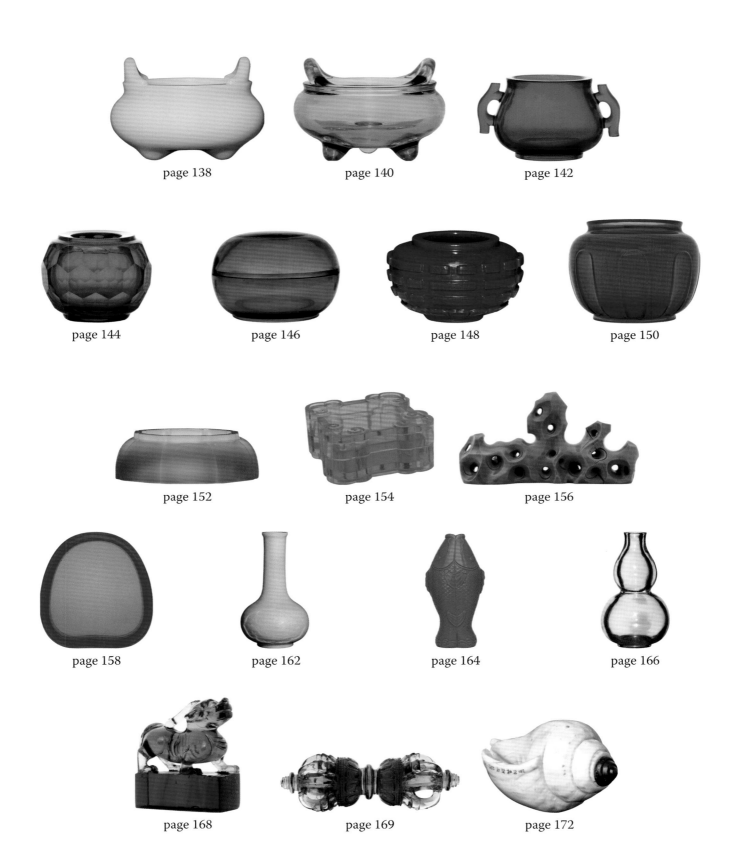

page 138

page 140

page 142

page 144

page 146

page 148

page 150

page 152

page 154

page 156

page 158

page 162

page 164

page 166

page 168

page 169

page 172

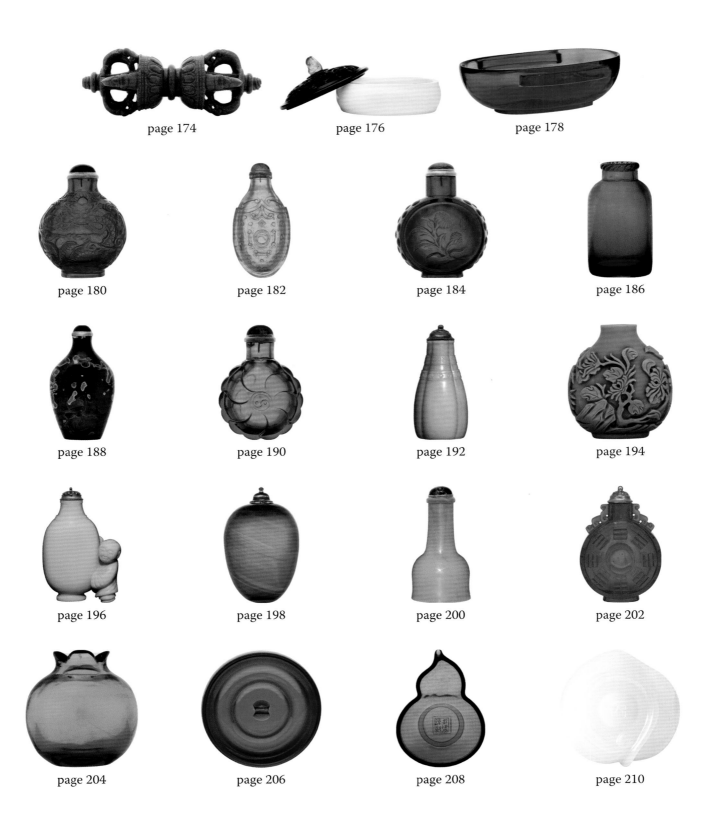

page 174

page 176

page 178

page 180

page 182

page 184

page 186

page 188

page 190

page 192

page 194

page 196

page 198

page 200

page 202

page 204

page 206

page 208

page 210

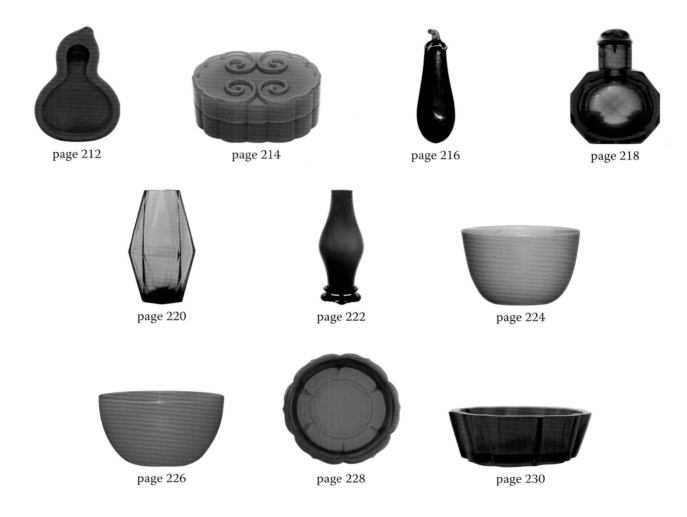

page 212

page 214

page 216

page 218

page 220

page 222

page 224

page 226

page 228

page 230